Network Computing Architecture

Lisa Zahn

Terence H. Dineen
Paul J. Leach
Elizabeth A. Martin
Nathaniel W. Mishkin
Joseph N. Pato
Geoffrey L. Wyant

Apollo Computer Inc.
a subsidiary of Hewlett-Packard Company
Chelmsford, Massachusetts

Prentice Hall
Englewood Cliffs, New Jersey 07632

Library of Congress Cataloging-in-Publication Data

Zahn, Lisa.
   Network computing architecture / Lisa Zahn ; Terence H. Dineen ...
[et al.].
      p.   cm.
   ISBN 0-13-611674-4
   1. Computer network architectures. 2. Computer network protocols.
I. Title.
TK5105.5.Z333   1989
004.6'5--dc20   89-38582
                                                             CIP

Editorial/production supervision: *Jacqueline A. Jeglinski*
Cover design: *Lundgren Graphics*
Manufacturing buyer: *Ray Sintel*

Published by Prentice-Hall, Inc.
A division of Simon & Schuster
Englewood Cliffs, New Jersey 07632

The publisher offers discounts on this book when ordered
in bulk quantities. For more information, write:

> Special Sales/College Marketing
> Prentice-Hall, Inc.
> College Technical and Reference Division
> Englewood Cliffs, NJ 07632

UNIX is a registered trademark of AT&T in the USA and other countries.

Printed in the United States of America
10 9 8 7 6 5 4 3 2 1

ISBN 0-13-611674-4

Prentice-Hall International (UK) Limited, *London*
Prentice-Hall of Australia Pty. Limited, *Sydney*
Prentice-Hall Canada Inc., *Toronto*
Prentice-Hall Hispanoamericana, S.A., *Mexico*
Prentice-Hall of India Private Limited, *New Delhi*
Prentice-Hall of Japan, Inc., *Tokyo*
Simon & Schuster Asia Pte. Ltd., *Singapore*
Editora Prentice-Hall do Brasil, Ltda., *Rio de Janeiro*

Contents

Chapter 4   NCA/RPC Packet Definition

Chapter 5   NCA/RPC Finite State Machine Definitions, Notations, and Conventions

Chapter 6   NCA/RPC Client Protocol Specification

Chapter 7   NCA/RPC Server Protocol Specification

Chapter 8   Conversation Manager Interface

Chapter 9   NIDL Grammar

Chapter 10   Network Data Representation

Chapter 11   NCA/LB Specification

Appendix A   NIDL yacc Input Specification

Appendix B   NCA Base Network Data Types

Appendix C   NCA Status Codes

Appendix D   ASCII/EBCDIC Conversion Tables

Glossary

Index

Figures

Tables

Preface

The Network Computing Architecture (NCA) is an architecture designed for the development of distributed applications. *Network Computing Architecture* provides protocol specifications for NCA components that systems architects and programmers can use when implementing NCA. The document defines and describes the following NCA components:

- The **NCA Remote Procedure Call (NCA/RPC)** facility, which extends the procedure call mechanism from a single–machine implementation to a distributed computing environment.

- The **Network Interface Definition Language (NIDL)**, which is a language designed for the specification of remote interfaces; that is, procedures to be invoked through the NCA/RPC mechanism.

- The **Network Data Representation** protocol **(NDR)**, which defines how the structured values supplied in a call to a remote interface are to be encoded into byte stream format for network transmission via NCA/RPC.

- The **Location Broker** protocol **(NCA/LB)**, which specifies the network interfaces for a highly available location service.

Organization of this Book

We've organized this book as follows:

Chapter 1   Introduces the NCA components.

Chapter 2   Describes the architectural concepts on which NCA is founded.

Chapter 3   Describes the network model that NCA employs.

Chapter 4   Defines the NCA/RPC packet structure.

Chapter 5   Defines the NCA/RPC finite state machine conventions and notations.

Chapter 6	Defines the NCA/RPC client protocol finite state machines.
Chapter 7	Defines the NCA/RPC server protocol finite state machine.
Chapter 8	Defines the NCA/RPC Conversation Manager interface.
Chapter 9	Describes NIDL syntax and semantics.
Chapter 10	Defines the NDR presentation protocol.
Chapter 11	Defines the NCA/LB network protocol.
Appendix A	Defines the NIDL grammar in **yacc** format.
Appendix B	Presents the NCA network base data type definitions (**nbase.idl**).
Appendix C	Presents the NCA status code definitions (**ncastat.idl**).
Appendix D	Presents ASCII/EBCDIC conversion tables.

A glossary and index appear after the appendixes.

Related Books

For information about the Network Computing System™ (NCS), an implementation of NCA developed by Apollo® Computer Inc., refer to the following documents, which we list with their Apollo order numbers:

- *Network Computing System Reference Manual* (010200)

- *Managing NCS Software* (011895)

- *Concurrent Programming Support (CPS) Reference* (010233)

The Apollo order number for *Network Computing Architecture* is 010201.

For information about the Berkeley UNIX* socket abstraction, refer to the following documents:

- *4.3BSD UNIX Programmer's Manual*

- *UNIX Programmer's Supplementary Documents, Volume 1 (PS1)*, 4.3 Berkeley Software Distribution

---

*UNIX is a registered trademark of AT&T in the USA and other countries.

Documentation Conventions

Unless otherwise noted in the text, this manual uses the following symbolic conventions.

literal values
Bold words or characters in formats and command descriptions represent commands or keywords that you must use literally. Pathnames are also in bold. Bold words in text indicate the first use of a new term. Bold keywords in FSM tables assume the meaning defined in Table 5–4.

user–supplied values
Italic words or characters in formats and command descriptions represent values that you must supply. Italic keywords in FSM tables assume the meaning defined in Table 5–4.

`output/source code`
Information that the system displays appears in this `typeface`. Examples of source code and NIDL grammar also appear in this `typeface`.

[   ]
Square brackets enclose optional items in formats and command descriptions. In sample NIDL statements, brackets assume their NIDL meanings.

{   }
Braces enclose a list from which you must choose an item in formats and command descriptions. In NIDL syntax descriptions, braces assume the meaning described in Table 9–1.

|
A vertical bar separates items in a list of choices.

<   >
Angle brackets enclose the name of a key on the keyboard. In NIDL syntax descriptions, angle brackets assume the meaning described in Table 9–1.

. . .
Horizontal ellipsis points indicate that you can repeat the preceding item one or more times.

.
.
.
Vertical ellipsis points mean that irrelevant parts of a figure or example have been omitted.

———— 🮒 ————
This symbol indicates the end of a chapter or part of a manual.

Lisa Zahn is a technical writer in the network computing group at Apollo Computer Inc.

Terence H. Dineen, Paul J. Leach, Elizabeth A. Martin, Nathaniel W. Mishkin, Joseph N. Pato, and Geoffrey L. Wyant are the designers of the Network Computing Architecture and the developers of the Network Computing System.

Chapter 1

An Overview of NCA

NCA (the Network Computing Architecture) is an architecture for building **distributed applications**; that is, applications that distribute both data *and* computation across a network of different machines. Distributed applications permit users to harness the collective computing power inherent in a network of heterogeneous systems and provide a way to make best use of the diverse resources available in a network. For example, a distributed application can consist of tools that permit applications to use the CPUs of several systems in parallel, or mechanisms that facilitate access to specialized processors.

The purpose of NCA is to serve as a building block for distributed applications. Its architecture addresses and solves the particular problems that distributed applications developers encounter in order to provide a reliable and portable platform for distributed application development.

Figure 1–1 illustrates the overall structure of NCA.

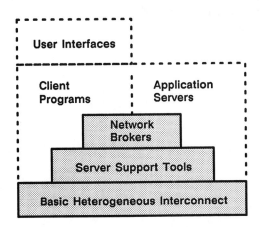

Figure 1-1. Structure of the Network Computing Architecture

NCA applies a client–server model to distributed applications. With this model, distributed applications are divided into client programs and application servers. **Client programs** are consumers of resources; **application servers** are the providers of those resources. For example, an application server can consist of software running on a specialized processor that offers high–performance array processing services; client programs make use of these services. NCA does not currently define any client program or application server protocols. Distributed applications can also include the user interfaces to the client programs. However, although user interfaces can be part of distributed applications, they are not part of NCA, and are thus not discussed in this document.

Client programs and application servers make use of network brokers, server support tools, and the heterogeneous interconnect. A **network broker** is a server that provides information about available resources, both local and network–wide. Brokers act as intermediaries between client programs requesting resources and the application servers that provide access to those resources. For example, a client program can query a network broker about the availability of a particular service it needs; the broker will locate an application server that provides the service and return the information to the client. Because network brokers provide a dynamic way to find and use new and changing resources, they permit the distributed application developer to concentrate on what the application is to do, rather than on where and how it is to be done.

The **server support tools** are packages of subroutines that simplify the development of complex applications in a distributed environment; for example, by handling replicated data or concurrent atomic transactions. The server support tools augment the basic heterogeneous interconnect and are also available to network brokers, client programs, and servers. NCA does not currently define any server support tools, although future versions of NCA may do so.

The basic **heterogeneous interconnect** is the lowest level of NCA, and provides the basic interconnection between heterogeneous computing systems. The remainder of this chapter introduces the components that NCA currently defines for the heterogeneous interconnect and network broker layers. Chapter 2 explains the architectural features on which these NCA components are based.

1.1 Heterogeneous Interconnect

The following components are currently defined at the heterogeneous interconnect level:

- The **NCA Remote Procedure Call (NCA/RPC)** facility, which extends the procedure call mechanism from a single–machine implementation to a distributed computing environment.

- The **Network Interface Definition Language (NIDL)**, which is a language designed for the specification of remote interfaces; that is, procedures to be invoked through the NCA/RPC mechanism.

- A **Network Data Representation** protocol (**NDR**), which defines how the structured values supplied in a call to a remote interface are to be encoded into byte stream format for network transmission via NCA/RPC.

This document provides specifications for these NCA components that systems architects and programmers can use when implementing NCA on their systems. The next sections discuss these components in more detail.

1.1.1 NCA Remote Procedure Call Facility

Remote Procedure Call (RPC) extends the procedure call mechanism from a single-machine implementation to a distributed computing environment: it permits an application program to call a procedure implemented in a server on a remote machine as if the procedure were local to the program. The **NCA Remote Procedure Call (NCA/RPC) facility** is NCA's implementation of the RPC mechanism. NCA/RPC is designed to use a low–cost protocol for the common remote procedure call and to be independent of the network communications protocols on top of which it is layered. To achieve these goals, NCA/RPC uses a network model that assumes an unreliable datagram service exists at the network layer, and it uses the Berkeley UNIX socket abstraction as the interface to this layer. Chapter 3 describes the NCA/RPC network model in more detail. The next sections describe NCA/RPC components and give a brief summary of NCA/RPC protocol operation.

1.1.1.1 NCA/RPC Components

Basic to all remote procedure call implementations is the exchange of request and response messages. The request message supplies information about the procedure to be executed and the procedure call's input parameters. The response message returns the call's output parameters, or an error indication if the call failed. NCA/RPC defines a **request–response protocol** and also defines a **packet format** that specifies how request and response messages are structured.

The request–response protocol is separated into client and server sides. The **client** is the software subsystem that implements the request–response protocol on the calling machine. The **server** is the software subsystem that implements the request–response protocol on the machine that implements the target remote procedure. Both client and server can be **multi–threaded**; that is, they can be implemented to handle multiple remote procedure calls simultaneously. In a multi–threaded implementation, client and server view each remote call as part of a thread of execution, called an **activity**.

NCA/RPC request–response protocol supports two types of remote call semantics: calls to idempotent operations and calls to non–idempotent operations. An **idempotent** operation is one that can be carried out more than once with no ill effect; that is, it does not modify the "state of the world" in an observable way. A **non–idempotent** operation is one that *cannot* be executed more than once because it either will return different results on each invocation or because it modifies some state.

1.1.1.2 NCA/RPC Protocol Summary

Client and server cooperate to execute a remote procedure call roughly as follows. The client sends a packet describing the call—a request packet—and waits for a response. The server receives the request, dispatches it for execution, and sends a packet in response that describes the results of executing the call (the response packet). If the client does not receive a response to a request within a particular amount of time, it can inquire about the status of the request by sending a **ping** packet. The server either sends back a **working** packet, indicating that execution of the request is in progress, or a **nocall** packet, which means that the request has been lost (or that the server has crashed and rebooted) and the client needs to resend it. Client and server are also able to fragment and reassemble requests or responses that are too large to fit in a single packet.

Because it does not matter whether an idempotent procedure is executed more than once, NCA/RPC makes no guarantees about how many times an idempotent procedure is executed. Consequently, if a called procedure is idempotent, the server is not required to save the results of the operation once it has sent back the response packet, nor is the client required to acknowledge its receipt. If the response is lost, the client will retransmit the request, and the server will execute it again and retransmit the response.

However, if a called procedure is not idempotent, NCA/RPC ensures that the server executes the call **at most once**; that is, zero or one times. On non–idempotent procedures, the server saves and periodically retransmits the response packet until the client has acknowledged receipt of the response. If the server receives a retransmission of the request, it resends the saved response instead of executing the call again. The client acknowledges the response either implicitly, by sending a new request, or explicitly, by sending an acknowledgment packet.

To detect duplicate requests for non–idempotent procedures, the server keeps track of the sequence number of the previous request for each client with which it has communicated. However, if the server has not heard from a client for some period of time (or has run out of storage space), it may discard this information. Thus, it is possible for a long–delayed duplicate request to arrive after the server has discarded information about the requesting client. To handle this case, the server "calls back" the client if it receives a non–idempotent request from a client about which it has no information. The **callback** is actually a call to an idempotent remote procedure in an NCA–defined interface that the client implements. The server requests the client's current sequence number in the callback, and uses the returned sequence number to validate the request. The callback mechanism also handles the case in which the server has executed the non–idempotent procedure but fails to send the response packet, either because of network partitions or a server crash.

Chapter 4 specifies NCA/RPC packet format and provides details about packet layout, semantics, and structure. Chapters 5 through 7 specify the client and server sides of the request–response protocol; Chapter 8 specifies the callback mechanism.

1.1.2 Network Interface Definition Language

An application program initiates the NCA/RPC protocol when it calls an operation in a remote interface. An **interface** is a set of related operations. Each operation is defined by its procedure or function name and its input and output parameters. A **remote interface** is a set of remote operations; that is, the callable operations within the interface are not necessarily local to the program that is calling them. The application uses the remote interface by making remote procedure calls to its operations.

NCA's **Network Interface Definition Language (NIDL)** is a language designed for the specification of remote interfaces; that is, procedures to be invoked through the NCA/RPC mechanism. The language consists of Pascal and C syntax and semantics that have been enhanced to address the special requirements of remote interface design. A remote **interface definition** written in NIDL contains information about the operations that can be called remotely and the number and type of their arguments. For each operation, the definition specifies the calling syntax that both the client and the remote operation will use during the remote procedure call.

The interface definition determines how NCA/RPC operates. It defines the request and response packet contents and the sequence of messages that make up the remote procedure call transaction given the called operation. For example, it is the interface definition that specifies whether or not an operation is idempotent, and thus controls which message sequence the client and server use to carry out the transaction.

The interface definition also determines a prototype NDR byte stream by virtue of the data types and operation parameters that it defines. The actual values and representation format for these data types and parameters, and hence, the actual contents of the byte stream, are supplied by the caller when it makes a call to an operation in the interface.

Chapter 9 specifies NIDL C (NIDL/C) and Pascal (NIDL/Pascal) syntax and describes NIDL semantics. The implementation of NCA is required to provide the code that compiles applications written in NIDL.

This specification uses NIDL syntax to describe NCA-defined data types and operations, including the following set of NCA-defined remote interfaces that all NCA implementations are required to support

- The Conversation Manager, defined in the interface definition file **conv.idl**. Chapter 8 describes the Conversation Manager and gives the complete contents of **conv.idl**.

- The Location Broker network interfaces, defined in the interface definition files **glb.idl** and **llb.idl**. Section 1.2 of this chapter describes the function of the Location Broker in NCA; Chapter 11 describes the Location Broker interfaces and gives the complete contents of the Global Location Broker (GLB) and Local Location Broker (LLB) interface definition files.

- A set of fundamental **base network data types** defined in the interface definition file **nbase.idl**. Chapters 2 and 3 describe the NCA base types that are central to an understanding of NCA protocols; Appendix B gives the complete contents of **nbase.idl**.

- The set of NCA network status messages, defined in the interface definition file **ncastat.idl**. Chapter 4 describes the set of network status messages transmitted as reject status from the server; Appendix C shows the definitions for all NCA status messages.

1.1.3 Network Data Representation

A remote procedure call architecture requires a data representation protocol to provide rules for:

- Encoding abstract values into a byte stream for transmission through a network.

- Handling heterogeneous forms of data representation so that machines with differing formats can communicate with one another.

NCA's data representation protocol is called **Network Data Representation (NDR)**. NDR specifies how structured values like records and arrays are to be encoded into byte stream format, and defines a way to represent scalar formats so that machines with different local representations can communicate typed values to each other. NDR is equivalent to the presentation layer in the International Organization for Standardization (ISO) Open Systems Interconnection (OSI) model of network communications protocols. The next sections introduce NDR mechanisms for data representation and conversion; Chapter 10 defines NDR protocol in full.

1.1.3.1 Data Representation Protocol

Programs treat data as structured values, such as integers, arrays, and records. Communications networks, on the other hand, treat data as a **byte stream,** which is a sequence of bytes indexed by non-negative integers. NDR's function is to define how the structured values in an application program's interface are to be represented in a byte stream. To this end, NDR defines a set of transmissible scalar data types and aggregate type constructors, which permits a mapping between an ordered set of typed values and a byte stream.

NDR must also handle the problem of differing kinds of data alignment across machine types. Many (although not all) machines recognize a basic data type and align data in memory based on this basic type. The basic data type recognized differs across CPU types; for example, a Motorola MC68000-based machine recognizes the 16-bit word as the basic data type and aligns data on 16-bit boundaries, while a VAX* machine recognizes the 32-bit longword as the basic type and aligns data on 32-bit boundaries. As a result, different machines will lay out a record, for example, in different ways in memory. If one CPU type is attempting to retrieve a record mapped into memory by a different CPU type, the operation to retrieve that data can be expensive or, in some cases, impossible.

NDR handles the issue of heterogeneous data alignment by requiring data to be naturally aligned in the byte stream. In **natural alignment,** scalar values of size 2^n are aligned at a byte stream index which is a multiple of 2^n up to some limiting value of n; NDR defines this limit to be three (that is, scalars of size up to eight bytes are naturally aligned). The use of natural alignment permits the use of natural operators to manipulate values in the byte stream efficiently and without alignment faults, and also promotes ease of communications between heterogeneous machine types.

Natural alignment means that fields within the NCA/RPC packet header and data in the packet body must be naturally aligned. Because natural alignment can lead to the creation of holes in a packet, the NCA/RPC packet header is structured to minimize the possibility of holes. However, it is the responsibility of the remote interface writer to declare data structures in an order that will minimize holes in the packet body, as NCA components do not reorder data to optimize packet size.

1.1.3.2 Data Conversion Protocol

Different computer architectures use different forms of data representation. For example, the order of bytes in an integer on a VAX machine is not the same as the order on a Motorola MC68000 machine. As a result, a remote procedure call architecture must handle the case of differing data representations between sending and receiving machines. Either the sending machine and the receiving machine must both agree to convert to and from a standard or **canonical** data representation format, or one or the other machine must convert the data from the foreign format to the format it understands.

---

* VAX is a registered trademark of Digital Equipment Corporation.

NDR uses a **multicanonical** approach to data conversion. Under this protocol, NDR defines a set of supported formats for character, integer, and floating–point scalars. Each sender uses one of the supported formats to encode its data into the byte stream; this format becomes the sender's native format. The sender then tags the byte stream with a **format label** that identifies the format in use; NDR defines this label as a 4–byte data structure. If the receiver determines from the format label that the incoming data is not in the format it uses as its native one, it converts the data to its native representation.

A multicanonical protocol means that no more than one conversion is ever needed, and then, only when there is a mismatch between sender and receiver. The cost of this approach is that every receiver must be prepared to transform incoming data in any supported format into its native format, and thus must maintain a record of all the types of data representation formats it might receive. Consequently, the set of representations that NDR supports is broadly useful but is not universal.

NDR does not define how the format label and the byte stream are stored in packets. Other NCA components, for example, NCA/RPC, comply with NDR when generating the format label and byte stream, encoding the format label in packet headers, fragmenting the byte stream into packet–sized pieces, and putting the fragments into packet bodies.

1.2 Network Broker Architecture

As mentioned earlier in this chapter, the NCA's network broker architecture is designed to permit the distributed application writer to concentrate on what the application is to do, rather than on where and how it is to be done. One aspect of this goal is the ability to provide location transparency; that is, to permit clients to determine a resource's location dynamically, and to allow programs to be designed without regard to whether their procedure calls result in local or remote execution. The **NCA Location Broker (NCA/LB)** is the network broker that supports this transparency.

The NCA/LB is a server process that enables a client to find specific resources, such as databases or remote interfaces. The NCA/LB keeps a database of available resources and their locations. If a client wants to locate a resource, it can interrogate the NCA/LB (via the NCA/RPC facility); the NCA/LB will return the locations of all the occurrences of that resource. Since the client can determine the locations of needed resources dynamically on demand from the NCA/LB, it does not require built–in, a priori knowledge of those resources' locations. Chapter 11 gives the protocol specification for the NCA/LB.

The NCA/LB is the first in a series of network brokers; future plans for extensions to the network broker architecture include an **attribute broker** that permits a client to specify the kind of service it needs, an **authentication broker** that provides secure communications between client and server, and a **power broker** that manages a pool of computers available for client computations.

Chapter 2

NCA Fundamentals

NCA is an **object-oriented** architecture; this means that its design is based on the concepts of object, object type, operation, and interface. NCA uses Universal Unique Identifiers, or UUIDs, to identify these entities. This chapter explains the object model and UUIDs in further detail.

2.1 The Object Model

In an object-oriented system, all resources in a network are characterized as **objects**. A disk file is an object, but so are named, non-disk resources such as devices and processes. Objects are organized into categories, or **types**. The type is used to separate the set of all objects into classes of like objects. Every object has a type; for example, a text file could have the type "unstructured ASCII," while an array processor could have the type "array processor."

Objects are manipulated by well-defined **operations**; an operation is like a procedure or a function. An **interface** is a set of related operations. Each object type has one or more interfaces associated with it. All accesses to a particular object are made through the operations defined in the interfaces associated with that object's type.

The object-oriented architecture maps onto the NCA/RPC client and server model as follows. A server handles some set of objects. It provides, or **exports,** all of the interfaces associated with those objects' types. A client uses the interfaces by making remote calls to the server that exports them; each remote call is made to a particular operation in an interface. The NIDL language further enforces this model by requiring that each call identify the object either implicitly or explicitly.

The NCA's object-oriented design is intended to encourage application designers to view remote calls as operations on objects (printers, files, compute engines, graphics displays), rather than viewing them as calls to particular machines or server processes. This approach to problem solving enables the designer to create programs that are less dependent on a site's hardware configuration, and are therefore less sensitive to changes in the configuration, for example, changes in the locations, names, and numbers of a site's special-purpose compute engines.

2.2 Universal Unique Identifiers

An important part of NCA's object-oriented model is its use of **Universal Unique Identifiers** to identify NCA entities such as objects, interfaces, and operations. A UUID is a fixed-length (16-byte) identifier that is guaranteed to refer to one entity for all time. A UUID is formed by combining the identity of the system that is generating the UUID with the current time on that system. NCA represents time as 48 bits of 4-microsecond ticks since January 1, 1980. It represents the system's (or **host's**) identity by combining its unique identifier, which is a **network address**, with a **protocol family identifier**, which specifies the communications protocol that created the host's network address. The protocol family identifier and host ID are elements of the network model that NCA uses; see Chapter 3 for a description of this model.

The 16 bytes of a UUID are organized as follows:

- The first six bytes hold the time the UUID was generated.

- The next two bytes are reserved.

- The next byte holds the protocol family ID.

- The next seven bytes hold the host ID in the format indicated by the protocol family.

NCA defines a base data type for the UUID; its representation, using NIDL/Pascal syntax, is as follows:

```
/* UUID Definition */

type
    uuid_$t =
        record
            time_high:  unsigned32;
            time_low:   unsigned;
            reserved:   unsigned;
            family:     byte;
            host:       array[1..7] of byte;
            end;
```

The UUID data type is a member of the set of base data types defined in the interface definition file **nbase.idl**. Appendix B gives the definitions of the set of NCA base data types, including the UUID, contained in **nbase.idl**.

There are several advantages to using UUIDs as low-level identifiers rather than using string names. UUIDs are of relatively smaller size and are easier to embed in data structures. UUIDs provide location transparency as well as the ability to layer various naming strategies on top of the primitive UUID naming mechanism. In addition, UUIDs can be generated anywhere without the need for prior contact with some other agent, for example, contact with a special server on the network, or a human representative of a company that hands out identifiers.

Chapter 3

NCA Network Model

NCA uses a network model that is derived from the Berkeley UNIX socket abstraction and which assumes that an unreliable datagram service exists at the network level. This chapter explain the motivations for this model.

3.1 Socket Abstraction

A network communications **protocol family** (or **address family**) is a set of related protocols; for example, Sequenced Packet Protocol (SPP) and Packet Exchange Protocol (PEP) are part of the Xerox* Network Systems (NS) protocol family, while Transmission Control Protocol (TCP) and User Datagram Protocol (UDP) are part of the Department of Defense (DoD) Internet Protocol (IP) family.

NCA is designed to be as independent of particular network communications protocol families as possible. To achieve this goal, NCA uses the Berkeley UNIX (BSD) socket abstraction as the communications layer underneath NCA/RPC. The socket abstraction masks the details of the various protocol families and also supports the concept of sending and receiving datagrams. Figure 3–1 illustrates the relationship between NCA components and the socket layer.

---

* Xerox is a registered trademark of the Xerox Corporation.

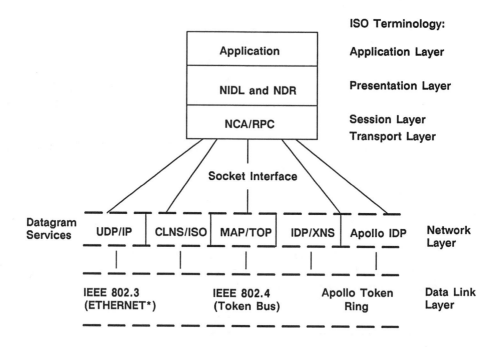

Figure 3-1. NCA and the Socket Abstraction

A **socket** is an endpoint of communications, in the form of a message queue. A server listens for incoming messages on a socket, while a client sends messages through a socket. A socket is uniquely identified by a **socket address**, which is a structure that contains a protocol family identifier, a network address, and a port number.

The **protocol family identifier** is a small number assigned by the University of California at Berkeley that specifies the protocol family that generated the network address. For example, a value of 6 indicates that the network address was generated using Xerox NS network address format.

---

* ETHERNET is a registered trademark of Xerox Corporation.

** TOP is a trademark of the Boeing Company.

The **network address** is a value that, given the protocol family, uniquely identifies a particular machine, or **host,** on a network.

A **port** refers to a socket message queue within a particular host. Each port is assigned a **port number** that distinguishes it from the other ports within the host. Clients and servers can make a special arrangement to communicate with each other through one specific port; a port used in this way is considered to be **well-known,** and the port number assigned to it will be identical across all hosts.

NCA defines a base socket address data type; the type is an opaque data structure that consists of

- The protocol family identifier (defined in the data type **socket_$addr_family_t**).

- A stream of bytes that contains a network address and a port number.

The type definition for the socket address, in NIDL/Pascal syntax, is as follows:

```
/* Socket Definition */

type
    socket_$addr_t = record
        family: socket_$addr_family_t;
        data:   array [0..13] of byte;
        end;

type
    socket_$addr_family_t = (
        socket_$unspec,
        socket_$unix,
        socket_$internet,
        socket_$implink,
        socket_$pup,
        socket_$chaos,
        socket_$ns,
        socket_$nbs,
        socket_$ecma,
        socket_$datakit,
        socket_$ccitt,
        socket_$sna,
        socket_$unspec2,
        socket_$dds
        );
```

The **socket_$addr_t** and **socket_$addr_family_t** data types are members of the set of base NCA data types defined in **nbase.idl.** Appendix B gives the definitions of these data types. Table 3-1 describes the set of protocol family identifiers that NCA defines in **socket_$addr_family_t.**

Table 3-1. Protocol Family Identifiers

Protocol Family	Identifier	Meaning
socket_$unspec	0	Unspecified protocol
socket_$unix	1	Local to host (UNIX pipes, portals)
socket_$internet	2	Internetwork protocols (TCP, UDP)
socket_$implink	3	ARPANET Interface Message Processor (IMP) addresses
socket_$pup	4	Xerox PARC Universal Packet (PUP) protocols (BSP, for example)
socket_$chaos	5	Massachusetts Institute of Technology (MIT) CHAOS protocols
socket_$ns	6	Xerox Network Systems (XNS) protocols
socket_$nbs	7	National Bureau of Standards (NBS) protocols
socket_$ecma	8	European Computer Manufacturers Association (ECMA)
socket_$datakit	9	Datakit protocols
socket_$ccitt	10	International Telegraph and Telephone Consultative Committee (CCITT) protocols (X.25, for example)
socket_$sna	11	IBM* Systems Network Architecture (SNA) protocols
socket_$unspec2	12	Unspecified protocol
socket_$dds	13	Apollo Domain®/Message (MSG) protocol

For more detailed information about the socket abstraction, see the *UNIX Programmer's Supplementary Documents, Volume 1 (PS1)*, 4.3 Berkeley Software Distribution.

---

* IBM is a registered trademark of International Business Machines Corporation.

3.2 Unreliable Datagram Service

A network environment has many aspects that are unpredictable or unreliable. For example, at the lowest level, network messages can be duplicated, lost, or delivered out of order, while remote computer systems can crash and reboot in the middle of performing a requested task. In contrast, there is little that is unpredictable or unreliable in a local procedure call — the procedure is simply executed once. From an application's perspective, a remote procedure call should look like a local procedure call. Consequently, the goal of an RPC protocol is to handle the unpredictable and unreliable aspects of networking to make remote procedure calls look as much like local procedure calls as possible.

One way to establish predictability and reliability in a network environment is to use a connection-oriented protocol as a transport layer underneath the RPC protocol. This type of transport protocol is designed to move long byte streams reliably; TCP/IP is an example of a connection-oriented protocol.

The alternate method for establishing predictability and reliability is to use an unreliable datagram service as the transport layer, and build the necessary features for predictability and reliability into the RPC protocol itself. In an **unreliable datagram service**, packet delivery is carried out on a "best effort" basis. Packets can be lost, duplicated, and can arrive in a different order from the one in which they were sent. An RPC protocol must handle these problems, as well as deal with server crashes. This is the approach that NCA uses. It assumes that an unreliable datagram exists as a transport layer, and implements the reliability it needs on top of this type of service. NCA uses this approach for the following reasons:

- To minimize message exchange and other overhead

- To provide predictable remote procedure call semantics

- To ensure that a transport layer is always present

The next sections describe these motivations in more detail.

3.2.1 Minimal Remote Call Overhead

A goal of NCA is to minimize the number of network packets that the client and server sides exchange during one remote call and other related RPC overhead. Connection-oriented protocols exact a high cost for connection setup and maintenance, both in terms of the number of messages exchanged and the amount of state required to maintain a connection. For example, most TCP/IP implementations exchange three messages to set up a TCP connection and three more to tear it down. With the addition of RPC request and response messages, a total of eight messages are exchanged to make a single remote call. Such a cost might be considered acceptable when a client is making a large number of calls to a single server. However, it becomes expensive if a client makes a series of single calls to a large number of servers. In addition, a popular server may need to handle calls from hundreds of clients within a short period of time (for example, one or two minutes). If the server uses a reliable connection, it must bear the cost of maintaining connection state for *all* of the clients. To avoid remote call overhead, NCA uses a connectionless protocol.

3.2.2 Predictable Remote Call Semantics

While the behavior of a single connection–oriented transport service with regard to remote call semantics is predictable, the behavior of such transport services across different protocol families and implementations is not. Certain features needed to implement standard procedure call semantics for RPC may be different depending on the implementation; in some cases, these features may not exist at all. For example, if one end of the connection crashes while no data is being written to it, does the process at the other end discover the crash right away? To implement the standard local procedure call semantics correctly, an exception should be raised in the calling process when the remote machine crashes. However, if the transport service does not signal the failure to the waiting client, the exception cannot be detected and raised.

The advantage of using an unreliable service instead of a connection–oriented protocol is that unreliable services tend to have common properties across dissimilar protocol families. The existence of a single RPC protocol on top ensures predictable RPC semantics across multiple protocol families and implementations.

3.2.3 Transport Layer Availability

In some cases, a connection–oriented protocol may not exist. For example, small embedded microprocessors used in real–time data acquisition environments may not be capable of supporting a full TCP/IP implementation. In contrast, unreliable services are often available in environments where reliable services are not. NCA assumes that any machine connected to a network will provide, at the least, an unreliable datagram service.

Chapter 4

NCA/RPC Packet Definition

NCA/RPC passes remote procedure call messages in **packets**. An NCA/RPC packet consists of a **packet header** and an optional data section, or **body**. The packet header contains protocol control information, while the packet body contains the call's input or output arguments. The definition of the NCA/RPC packet in NIDL/C syntax is shown below.

```
/* Packet Definition */

typedef struct {
   nca_rpc_$pkt_t    header;
   byte              [last_is(header.len)] body[];
   }
nca_rpc_$pkt_t;
```

In practice, the size of a packet is limited to the datagram size that a particular datagram service supports. For example, if NCA/RPC is layered on top of a datagram service that can only send and receive 1–KB datagrams, then the NCA/RPC packet size is limited to 1 KB. If the datagram service does not impose a limit on the size of a datagram, NCA permits a packet whose total maximum length is 80 bytes (the packet header) plus 65536 bytes (the packet body). Note that the maximum packet body size is not necessarily the total length of the request, as the protocol will fragment large requests into multiple packets. The maximum number of fragments is defined by the size of the fragment number header field and is 65536.

4.1 Packet Header

This specification defines NCA/RPC packet header fields as abstract data types in a fictitious NIDL/C interface definition named **nca_rpc,** which is shown below. Note that the packet header is padded to a multiple of 8 bytes to ensure that the beginning of the packet body is naturally aligned.

```
/* Packet Header Interface Definition */

interface nca_rpc;
import
    'nbase.idl';

/* packet types */
        const int nca_rpc_$pt_request  = 0;
        const int nca_rpc_$pt_ping     = 1;
        const int nca_rpc_$pt_response = 2;
        const int nca_rpc_$pt_fault    = 3;
        const int nca_rpc_$pt_working  = 4;
        const int nca_rpc_$pt_nocall   = 5;
        const int nca_rpc_$pt_reject   = 6;
        const int nca_rpc_$pt_ack      = 7;
        const int nca_rpc_$pt_quit     = 8;
        const int nca_rpc_$pt_fack     = 9;
        const int nca_rpc_$pt_quack    = 10;

/* packet flags */

        const int nca_rpc_$pf_forwarded   = 16#0001;
        const int nca_rpc_$pf_last_frag   = 16#0002;
        const int nca_rpc_$pf_frag        = 16#0004;
        const int nca_rpc_$pf_no_fack     = 16#0008;
        const int nca_rpc_$pf_maybe       = 16#0010;
        const int nca_rpc_$pf_idempotent  = 16#0020;
        const int nca_rpc_$pf_broadcast   = 16#0040;

/* data representation format label */

typedef
    byte nca_rpc_$drep_t[4];
```

```
/* NCA/RPC packet header */

typedef struct {
    unsigned small   rpc_vers,      /* NCA/RPC version no. */
    unsigned small   ptype,         /* Packet type */
    unsigned small   flag,          /* Packet flags */
    byte             pad1,          /* Pad to 0 mod 4-byte boundary */
    nca_rpc_$drep_t  drep,          /* Data representation of sender */
    uuid_$t          object,        /* Object identifier */
    uuid_$t          if_id,         /* Interface identifier */
    uuid_$t          actuid,        /* Activity identifier */
    unsigned long    server_boot,   /* Server boot time */
    unsigned long    if_vers,       /* Interface version */
    unsigned long    seq,           /* Sequence number */
    unsigned short   opnum,         /* Operation in interface */
    unsigned short   ihint          /* Interface hint */
    unsigned short   ahint,         /* Activity hint */
    unsigned short   len,           /* Length of packet body */
    unsigned short   fragnum        /* Fragment number */
    byte             pad2           /* Pad to 0 mod 8-byte boundary */
}
    nca_rpc_$pkt_hdr_t;
```

The bit layout of a particular header field is determined by

- The field's type definition

- The way in which NDR represents that type in a byte stream

- The local data representation format, which is one of the supported integer, character, and floating-point formats defined by NDR

To illustrate how type definition, NDR byte stream representation, and local data representation format define bit layout, consider the object identifier field in the packet header. This field is an abstract data type of **uuid_$t**. This data type is defined (in **nbase.idl** in NIDL/Pascal) as a record type, as follows:

```
type
    uuid_$t =
        record
            time_high:   unsigned32;
            time_low:    unsigned;
            reserved:    unsigned;
            family:      byte;
            host:        array[1..7] of byte;
        end;
```

NDR represents the record data type by the representations of its fields in the order in which the record defines them. The number of bytes required to encode each field is determined by each field's type. In the case of **uuid_$t**, the first three fields are a long integer and two short integers. (NCA defines the data type sizes for short integers and long integers to be 16 bits and 32 bits, respectively.) Consequently, NDR represents **time_high** as an unsigned binary number encoded in four consecutive bytes, represents **time_low** and **reserved** as unsigned binary numbers encoded in two consecutive bytes each, and encodes **family** as one uninterpreted byte. Because NDR requires natural alignment, there may be gaps between fields. Since the **uuid_$t** type is naturally aligned, there are no gaps between its fields.

The local integer representation format (big–endian or little–endian) determines the integers' most–significant and least–significant bytes. If the local format is **big–endian**, the bytes of the representation are ordered in consecutive bytes from most–significant byte to least–significant byte. If the integer format is **little–endian**, the bytes of the representation are ordered in consecutive bytes from least–significant byte to most–significant byte.

The **host** data type is a fixed array of the NIDL **byte** type. NDR represents a fixed array in the byte stream as an ordered sequence of element representations; it represents each element value according to the array's element type. As a result, NDR encodes **host** in seven consecutive bytes.

Chapter 10 defines the set of NDR representations for structured values in byte stream format. It also defines the set of supported formats for character, integer, and floating–point values. The remainder of this chapter gives the meanings of the fields within the packet header and illustrates the different types of packet structures. The remainder of this section describes the semantics of the packet header.

4.1.1 Protocol Version Number

The **protocol version number** is an 8–bit non–negative integer that identifies the NCA/RPC version. This field is modified at each new release of the protocol. Its purpose is to keep track of multiple versions of the protocol that may exist in a distributed environment, where a server and a client may be using different versions of NCA/RPC. Its value should be 4.

4.1.2 Packet Type

The **packet type** field is an 8–bit non–negative integer that identifies the kind of request the client is making or the kind of response the server is returning. Table 4–1 describes the packet types that NCA supports.

Table 4-1. Packet Types

Type	Direction	Value	Meaning
request	client to server	0	The client requests execution of a remote operation.
ping	client to server	1	The client requests acknowledgment of an outstanding request.
response	server to client	2	The server is returning the results of a requested remote operation.
fault	server to client	3	The remote operation that the client requested incurred a fault during execution on the server.
working	server to client	4	The server is processing the request.
nocall	server to client	5	The server has no record of the client's request.
reject	server to client	6	The server has rejected the client's request for execution of a remote operation.
ack	client to server	7	The client has received the response to its request for execution of a non–idempotent remote operation.
quit	client to server	8	The client has requested that the server abort the execution of a remote call request.
fack	both ways	9	The client has received a response fragment (client to server) or the server has received a request fragment (server to client).
quack	server to client	10	The server has received a client quit request.

4.1.3 Flags

The flags field is an 8–bit integer that defines bit flags used in protocol control. Table 4–2 lists the NCA/RPC packet flags.

Table 4–2. Packet Flags

Name	Hex Value	Meaning if Set
reserved	01	Reserved. Do not use.
lastFrag	02	Indicates that the packet is a fragment of a multipacket transmission.
nofack	04	Indicates that the receiver should not send a fack packet for the fragment.
maybe	10	Directs the client and server FSMs to use the maybe protocol. This flag is set if the operation being called specifies the **maybe** routine attribute. See Chapter 9 for more information about routine attributes.
idempotent	20	Directs the client and server FSMs to use the idempotent protocol. This flag is set if the operation being called specifies the **idempotent** routine attribute. See Chapter 9 for more information about routine attributes.
broadcast	40	Directs the client and server FSMs to use the broadcast protocol. This flag is set if the operation being called specifies the **broadcast** routine attribute. See Chapter 9 for more information about routine attributes.

4.1.4 Data Representation Format Label

The **data representation format label** is a vector of four bytes that identifies the integer, character, and floating–point formats that the sender has used in the packet body. NCA/RPC defines the format label in the packet header as the data type **nca_rpc_$drep_t**. The packet format label supports the NDR multicanonical data conversion protocol for transmitting heterogeneous data representation. Under this protocol, NDR supports a set of data representation formats for integer, character, and floating–point values. See Chapter 10 for a discussion of the supported NDR data representation formats and how they are represented in the format label.

In addition to describing the sender's data, the format label also serves as a description of the integer format that the sender has used for the packet header. NCA/RPC uses the label as a conversion signal upon receipt of the packet. If the system receiving the incoming packet supports a different integer format from the one indicated in this field, it must convert the packet header in order to read the rest of the information it contains.

4.1.5 Object Identifier

The **object identifier** is a UUID that uniquely identifies the object to which the call is referring, if the call is operating on an object. If the call does not operate on an object, this field contains 0s. See Chapter 2 for a definition of object and UUID.

4.1.6 Interface Identifier

The **interface identifier** is a UUID that uniquely identifies the interface that the client is calling. The server uses the object UUID, interface UUID, the interface version number, and the operation number to decide which operation to call on the client's behalf. See Chapter 2 for the definition of interface and UUID.

4.1.7 Activity Identifier

The **activity identifier** is a UUID that uniquely identifies the client activity that is making the remote procedure call. The server can use the activity UUID as a communications key between it and a particular client by saving the activity UUIDs it receives from clients, thus keeping a record of all the activities with which the server is communicating. See Chapter 2 for a complete description of UUID format.

4.1.8 Server Boot Time

Server boot time is a 32–bit non–negative integer that indicates the time at which the server last booted; that is, the time at which this incarnation of the server was initiated (not the time at which the machine was last booted). Server boot time is represented as time in seconds since January 1, 1970 and must be increased monotonically every time the server boots. The server inserts its boot time into this field in all packets that it sends to a client. The client then uses this value on subsequent remote calls to the same server. The client will not have a server's boot time unless it has previously communicated with the server; if the client does not have the server's boot time, it inserts 0 into this field. The purpose of the server boot time is to ensure that non–idempotent procedures are not executed more than once in the face of a server crash; the rules for its use are specified in the NCA/RPC client and server specifications (Chapters 5 through 7) and in the Conversation Manager interface (Chapter 8).

4.1.9 Interface Version

The **interface version** is a 32–bit non–negative integer that identifies the version number of the interface being called. It allows servers to implement multiple versions of a single interface. On a call to a remote operation, this field will contain the interface version number specified in the target interface definition header; see Chapter 9 for a description of this structure.

4.1.10 Sequence Number

The **sequence number** field is a 32–bit non–negative integer that identifies the remote call that an activity is making. Each remote call that an activity makes has a unique sequence number that is assigned when the call is initiated. All NCA/RPC messages issued on behalf of a single remote call will have the same sequence number (whether messages are from client to server, or server to client). Each time the activity initiates a *new* remote request, it increases the sequence number so that each subsequent call has a larger sequence number. Together, the sequence number and the activity UUID uniquely identify a remote call. No two distinct remote calls can have the same activity UUID/sequence number pair.

4.1.11 Operation Number

The **operation number** is a 16–bit non–negative integer that identifies a particular operation within an interface. On a call to a remote operation, this field will contain the number of the target operation within the interface. (Operations are numbered in the order in which they are defined in the interface, starting with 0).

4.1.12 Interface Hint

The **interface hint** is a 16–bit non–negative integer. Although the server can use this field for any purpose, its intended use is to provide a way to optimize server interface lookups. When the server executes a call on a client's behalf, it can use this field to return information to the client that indicates which interface within the server is being called. The client can then pass this interface "hint" back to the server on subsequent calls to the same interface; the assumption is that this information will save the overhead of a lookup operation on the interface. If the server uses this field, it must be able to verify incoming values within it. It is suggested that the client insert the value FFFF(hex) into the interface hint field if it has no value from prior contact with the server.

4.1.13 Activity Hint

The **activity hint** is a 16–bit non–negative integer. Although the server can use this field for any purpose, its intended use is to provide a way to optimize activity ID lookup by a server that implements the handling of simultaneous client requests. When the server executes a call on a client's behalf, it can use this field to return information to the client that identifies the activity making the call. The client can then pass back this activity "hint" on subsequent remote calls to the same server. If the server uses this field, it must be able to verify incoming values within it. It is suggested that the client insert the value FFFF(hex) into the activity hint field if it has no value from prior contact with the server.

4.1.14 Packet Body Length

The **packet body length** is a 16-bit non-negative integer that indicates the length of the packet's data section; for example, the call's input or output arguments, in bytes. The maximum packet body size is 65535 bytes $(2^{16}-1)$.

4.1.15 Fragment Number

The **fragment number** is a 16-bit non-negative integer that identifies a packet when it is part of a multipacket transmission. NCA/RPC uses the fragment number field when a remote call has more input or output data than can fit into one packet. It acts as a sub-sequence number to identify separate packets (called fragments) in long transmissions; the protocol increases the fragment number monotonically for each fragment of the transmission. Each separate packet has a unique fragment number, but all the packets in the transmission have the same sequence number.

4.2 Packet Structure

A packet's structure depends upon its packet type, as discussed in Section 4.1.2. Packet types can be grouped into packets that the client sends and packets that the server sends. Packets that the client sends are request, ping, ack, and quit. Packets that the server sends are response, fault, reject, nocall, quack, and working. Both client and server send fack packets. All packet fragments that the client sends are labeled as request packets, while all packet fragments that the server sends are labeled as response packets.

4.2.1 Client-Initiated Packet Structures

Table 4-3 describes the packets that the client initiates.

Table 4–3. Client–Initiated Packets

Packet Type	Description
request	The client sends a request packet when it wants to execute a remote call. The request packet is composed of the packet header and the input arguments that the remote procedure requires. Request packets have idempotent, broadcast, maybe, broadcast/maybe, and non–idempotent (at most once) subtypes. These request packet subtypes are defined in Table 4–4. In a multipacket transmission of a client request, the client request consists of a series of request packets with the same sequence number and monotonically increasing fragment numbers.
ping	The client sends a ping packet when it wants to inquire about an outstanding request. A ping packet has no input arguments and so consists of the packet header only.
ack	The client sends an acknowledgment (ack) packet after it has received a response packet to a non–idempotent request (see Table 4–4). An ack packet is an explicit acknowledgment to the server that the client has received the response, and is the server's signal to cease resending the response and discard the packet. (A server will also stop resending a response packet once it receives a new request from the client.)
fack	The client sends a fragment acknowledgment (fack) packet after it receives one fragment of a multipacket response. A fack packet is an explicit acknowledgment to the server that the client has received the fragment, and is the server's signal to send the next fragment of the response. The server may inhibit the sending of facks by setting the nofack packet flag bit in the packet flags field.
quit	The client sends a quit packet when it has incurred a quit fault. The quit packet informs the server that it is to abort processing of the remote call.

Table 4–4. Client Request Packet Subtypes

Request Type	Meaning
idempotent	The request is for an idempotent procedure. Idempotent requests have the idempotent bit flag set in the packet flags field.
broadcast	The request is for an idempotent procedure to be sent to all servers in the network. A broadcast request has the broadcast bit flag set in the packet flags field. Note that the size of a broadcast packet is a function of the datagram service in use.
maybe	The request is for an idempotent procedure to which the client does not expect a response. Note that the maybe protocol does not guarantee that the receiving side has actually received the request. A maybe request has the maybe bit flag set in the packet flags field.
broadcast/maybe	The request is for an idempotent procedure to which the client does not expect a response and which is to be sent to all servers in the network. A broadcast/maybe request has the broadcast and the maybe bit flags set in the packet flags field.
at most once	The request is for a procedure that cannot be executed more than once. A non–idempotent request is the default request (it has no bit flags set).

4.2.2 Server–Initiated Packet Structures

Any packet field that is not defined to have meaning in a server–initiated packet must contain the same value as that passed in the client–initiated packet; that is, the server can change the packet type, body, fragment Booleans and variables, hints, and boot time, but it must preserve all other client packet values. Note that the server does not send response packets for requests that indicate the maybe protocol.

Table 4–5 describes the server–initiated packet types.

Table 4–5. Server–Initiated Packets

Packet Type	Description
response	The server sends a response packet if the procedure executed successfully. The response packet is composed of the packet header and the output arguments generated by the remote procedure execution. In a multi-packet transmission of a server response, the response consists of a series of response packets with the same sequence number and monotonically increasing fragment numbers.
working	The server sends a working packet as a reply to a client ping packet; this reply indicates that the server is processing the remote call. A working packet has no input arguments and so consists of the packet header only.
nocall	The server sends a nocall packet as a reply to a client ping packet; the reply indicates that the server has no record of the client's call in its database. A nocall packet consists of the packet header only.
fault	The server sends a fault packet if the remote call received a fault while executing on the server side. A fault packet body contains the fault status that corresponds to the fault that occurred.
reject	The server sends a reject packet if it has rejected the client's request. A reject packet body contains a specific reject status message; the set of reject status messages is defined in Table 4–6.
fack	The server sends a fragment acknowledgment (fack) packet after it receives one fragment of a multipacket request. A fack packet is an explicit acknowledgment to the client that the server has received the fragment, and is the client's signal to send the next fragment of the request. The client may inhibit the sending of facks by setting the nofack packet flag bit in the packet flags field.
quack	The server sends a quit acknowledgment (quack) packet after it has received a client quit packet. The quack packet is an explicit acknowledgment to the client that the server has aborted the remote call intended for execution on the client's behalf.

Table 4-6. Reject Status Codes

Name	Value (Hex)	Meaning
OprOutOfRange	1C010002	The presented operation number is greater than the number of operations in the interface, minus 1.
UnknownInterface	1C010003	The server does not export the requested interface.
WrongBootTime	1C010006	The server boot time passed in the packet does not match the server's record of its boot time.
ProtocolError	1C01000B	The client or server FSM protocol has been violated.
OutArgsTooBig	1C010013	The remote operation's output arguments have overflowed the buffer that the server reserved for it.
UnsupportedType	1C010017	The requested operation is not implemented for the type of object to which the operation is being applied.
ZeroDivide	1C000001	The remote operation incurred a divide-by-zero error during execution on the server.
AddressError	1C000002	The remote operation incurred an address exception during execution on the server.
FpDivZero	1C000003	The remote operation incurred a floating-point divide-by-zero error while executing on the server.
FpUnderflow	1C000004	The remote operation incurred a floating-point underflow error while executing on the server.
FpOverflow	1C000005	The remote operation incurred a floating-point overflow error while executing on the server.

Chapter 5

NCA/RPC Finite State Machine Definitions, Notations, and Conventions

NCA/RPC request–response protocol is divided into client and server sides. This specification defines the client and server protocols as **Finite State Machines (FSMs)**; the client consists of four FSMs, while the server consists of one FSM. Client and server FSMs are designed to operate together; that is, the output of the client FSMs is the input to the server FSM, and the output of the server FSM is intended for the client FSMs.

Chapters 6 and 7 specify the client and server FSMs, respectively. This chapter provides the FSM definitions used in client and server specifications and describes the notations and conventions used in the state transition tables that appear in Chapters 6 and 7.

5.1 Definitions

An FSM defines a set of states, inputs, and state transitions. An FSM has a **current state** which changes as a result of inputs. The **new state** is determined by reference to the set of valid possible state transitions. A **state transition** is a tuple [state, input, condition, new state, action]. The **condition** is a Boolean expression whose terms are discussed below. A transition is considered possible only if the condition is true. All the transitions for a single state are ordered. For an FSM in state S, upon input I, the new current state becomes the new state from the first possible transition of the form [S, I, ...], and the action from that transition is executed.

5.1.1 Inputs

FSM **inputs** can be

- **Messages**. Message inputs occur when NCA/RPC packets arrive. The set of messages is the set of NCA/RPC packet types. Packet types are defined in Table 4–1.

- **Timeouts**. Timeout inputs are associated with certain states, and occur after a certain amount of time has passed in that state with no other inputs. The set of client timeouts is defined in Table 6–1. The set of server timeouts is defined in Table 7–1.

- **Client actions** or **server execution engine notifications**. Client actions are either the initiation of a remote call (*ClientCall*) or a request to terminate a call in progress (*ClientQuit*).

  Execution engine notifications are generated by server FSM actions that invoke an execution engine. The **execution engine** is the model for the execution of a remote operation; the engine performs computations on the server FSM's behalf and returns results (if any) as notification input to the FSM. Execution engine **notification input** occurs as the result of FSM calls to the execution engine, and indicates that the execution engine has changed its state. Notification inputs are listed in Table 7–2. Server FSM primitives that invoke the execution engine are described in Table 7–6 and defined in Section 7.8.

5.1.2 Input Bundles

Message, client action, and server execution engine notification inputs have structured **bundles** of data associated with them. The nature of the data in a bundle depends on the type of FSM input.

The bundle associated with message input consists of

- NCA/RPC packet header field values, as described in Section 4.1. Table 5–1 lists the packet field bundle data and the header fields to which they correspond.

- NCA/RPC flag values, as described in Table 4–2. A packet flag value in a message input bundle indicates a Boolean expression which is true only if the named flag is set in the packet header. Table 5–2 lists packet flag bundle data.

- The source address of the message sender, which is a socket address, as defined in **nbase.idl** and described in Chapter 3. The source address bundle data identifies the location from which the message input originated.

- The NCA/RPC packet body, which contains the call's input or output parameters.

Table 5-1. Packet Header Bundle Data

Part of Bundle	Packet Field Value
[activityID]	The UUID specified in the activity ID field in the packet header of the message.
[bootTime]	The time specified in the server boot time field in the packet header of the message.
[ifID]	The UUID specified in the interface ID field in the packet header of the message.
[fragNum]	The integer specified in the fragment number field in the packet header of the message.
[opNum]	The integer specified in the operation number field in the packet header of the message.
[seqNum]	The integer specified in the sequence number field in the packet header of the message.

Table 5–2. Packet Flag Bundle Data

Part of Bundle	Packet Field Value
[broadcast]	The broadcast flag in the flags field of the message's packet header is set.
[frag]	The fragment flag in the flags field of the message's packet header is set.
[idempotent]	The idempotent flag in the flags field of the message's packet header is set.
[lastFrag]	The last fragment flag in the flags field of the message's packet header is set.
[maybe]	The maybe flag in the flags field of the message's packet header is set.
[nofack]	The nofack flag in the flags field of the message's packet header is set.

The bundle associated with client action input depends upon whether the input is a *ClientCall* or *ClientQuit*. Table 6–3 defines the bundle data associated with client action inputs.

The bundle associated with execution engine notification input is a function of the notification returned by the execution engine; notification bundles are described in Table 7–3.

5.1.3 Conditions

Conditions are functions of

- **Constants**. Client FSM constants are defined in Table 6–5. Server FSM constants are defined in Table 7–4.

- **Global variables**. Global variables can be modified by transition actions. Client global variables are defined in Table 6–6. Server global variables are defined in Table 7–5.

- The bundle associated with the FSM input.

Constants, global variables, and bundles have associated types (integer, Boolean). Integer terms can be compared by using relational operators (=, >, and so on) to yield Boolean values. A term consisting of a single packet header flag yields true if and only if the flag is set in the current message input.

5.1.4 Actions

Actions are executed as a result of state transitions. Steps within an action are represented as

- Primitive global variable assignments.

- Calls to client primitives or server execution engine primitives. The syntax for the primitives follows the description of the FSMs.

Both global variable assignments and primitive calls can refer to the constants, global variables, and bundles defined in client or server FSMs. The special operators defined in Table 5–3 can be used in global variable assignments.

Table 5–3. Special Operators

Operator	Example	Meaning
++	fragNum++	Increment value of global variable.
NULL	inParams := NULL	Assign an array of bytes whose length is equal to 0.
$\oplus$	inParams := inParams $\oplus$ [body]	Append two arrays of bytes together.
StatustoNDR()	StatustoNDR([rejectStatus])	Convert status code to an array of bytes in NDR format.
NDRtoStatus()	NDRtoStatus([body])	Convert an array of bytes in NDR format to a status code.

5.2 Notations

This section defines the notation used in FSM state transition tables, action tables, and the text of this specification to indicate FSM components. It also defines a notation for fragmentation.

5.2.1 Component Notation

Table 5–4 summarizes the notation used for client and server FSM state, input, condition, and action components.

Table 5–4. FSM Component Notation

Component	Notation	Example
Message input	*message*	*request*
Client action/notification input	*InputEvent*	*ClientCall*
State	**state**	**in_reply**
Global Variable	globVar	quitCount
Constant	SomeConstant	MaxBodyLen
Timeout input	@NameofTimeout	@QuitTimeout
Bundle data	[partOfBundle]	[inFragNum]
Action	*action*	*frag ack*

5.2.2 Fragment Notation

A **fragment** is a consecutive string of data bytes whose length cannot exceed the client and server FSM constant MaxBodyLen. A client call whose input data is larger than MaxBodyLen is sent in multiple fragments from the client to the server. An operation whose output data is larger than MaxBodyLen is sent in multiple fragments from the server to the client. The notation *data[n]* indicates the *n*th fragment in a string of bytes, *data* (zero–based).

The number of fragments of a given input or output data buffer is determined by the function

lengthInFrags = (length in bytes of buffer / (MaxBodyLen – sizeof(PacketHeader)))

This function is represented in FSM tables by the notation lengthInFrags(buffer), where buffer is client input data or server output data.

5.3 FSM Table Conventions

The client FSM state transitions and actions are given in Tables 6-8 through 6-15. The server FSM state transitions and actions are given in Tables 7-7 and 7-8. The client and server FSM tables use the following conventions:

- Each line of an FSM table specifies a state transition. From left to right, it shows the current state, the input event, the condition(s) in force (if any), and the resulting state and action generated (if any).

- Actions are given symbolic names under the Actions column in the FSM table and are enumerated in a separate table.

- The slash character (/) under Input indicates that no input has occurred; under Condition, that there is no applicable timeout or condition; under Action, that no action occurs.

- When the message in Input has associated data, that data can be referred to in the action associated with the transition line.

- A null Input field (/) acts as a pre-condition to entering the state. The associated condition is checked before transitioning to the state, and a state transition can occur even though there is no input.

- When more than one action is to be performed, the actions are separated by a semicolon (;).

Chapter 6

NCA/RPC Client Protocol
Specification

The NCA/RPC client protocol consists of four FSMs:

- A **send–await–reply (SAR)** FSM that handles client requests for idempotent and non–idempotent remote procedure execution.

- A **broadcast** FSM that handles client requests for remote procedure calls to be sent to all servers on a local network. A broadcast request must be to an idempotent procedure.

- A **maybe** FSM that handles remote procedure call requests from clients who do not expect to receive responses. A maybe request must be to an idempotent procedure.

- A **broadcast/maybe** FSM that handles client requests for "maybe" remote procedure calls to be broadcast to all servers on a local network. A broadcast maybe request must be to an idempotent procedure.

In addition to implementing the four finite state machines, the client must also listen for server callback requests and must implement and export the Conversation Manager interface that processes these requests. The **Conversation Manager** is a.remote interface written in NIDL that the server FSM calls to ensure the "at most once" rule for execution of non–idempotent procedures. Chapter 8 describes the Conversation Manager.

The remainder of this chapter defines the timeouts, input bundles, constants, global variables, and primitives used in the client FSMs and gives FSM transition tables and action descriptions for the four FSMs.

6.1 Response Message Acceptance Criteria

Before a client FSM accepts an incoming packet as FSM message input, the packet must satisfy the following criteria:

- The incoming packet's activity ID matches the activity ID associated with the outstanding request.

- The packet's server boot time matches the client's record of the server boot time unless the client has no record of a server boot time.

The client FSMs assume that all incoming packets have met these default acceptance conditions.

6.2 Client Timeouts

Table 6–1 describes the timeouts accepted as input to the client FSMs.

Table 6-1. Client Timeouts

Timeout	State	Suggested Time in State	Meaning
@AckTimeout	done	3 seconds	How long the client will wait before sending an ack packet.
@BrdcstTimeout	wait	5 seconds	How long the client will wait for a response to a broadcast request packet.
@FragTimeout	fack_wait	1 second	How long the client will wait for a fack after having sent a fragment of a request.
@PingWaitTimeout	ping_wait	1 second	How long the client will wait for a response to a ping packet.
@QuitTimeout	quit_wait	1 second	How long the client will wait for a response to a quit packet.
@WaitTimeout	wait	see Note	How long the client will wait for a response to a request packet.

Note: The number of seconds, T, that passes in the wait state before a @WaitTimeout input occurs is a function of the waitCount global variable. T is computed to be 2 ** min(10, waitCount). The client pings soon after having sent a request, but less frequently as the execution progresses.

6.3 Client Actions

Table 6-2 describes the client actions.

Table 6-2. Client Actions

Event	Meaning
ClientCall	The client has issued a remote call. The bundle data associated with the *ClientCall* action are [CallSpec], [idempotent], and [inParams].
ClientQuit	The client has issued a request to terminate a call in progress. The input bundle associated with the *ClientQuit* action is [callSpec].

6.4 Client Action Input Data

Table 6-3 describes the bundle data associated with client action FSM input.

Table 6-3. Client Action Bundle Data

Bundle/Notation	Type	Meaning
[callSpec]	array of bytes	The call specification (in NDR format) associated with the client action. Table 6-4 defines the contents of [callSpec].
[idempotent]	Boolean	A Boolean value associated with the *ClientCall* action that is true only if the call is to an idempotent procedure.
[inParams]	array of bytes	The input parameters associated with the *ClientCall* action.

Table 6-4. Call Specification Bundle Data Contents

Bundle Contents	Meaning
if_id	The UUID of the target interface, as specified in the interface header **uuid** attribute.
if_vers	The version number of the target interface, as specified in the interface header **version** attribute.
port_list	A vector of port numbers indexed by address family, as specified in the **port** attribute in the target interface header. Note that a port within a list can have the value "unspecified".
object	The UUID of the target object; this value is passed in the handle parameter specified in the remote call.
location	The object location information passed in the handle parameter specified in the remote call. The location information is in the form of a socket address, as defined in Chapter 3 (**socket_$addr_t**) and in **nbase.idl**.
opnum	A 32-bit integer that identifies the target operation's number within the interface.

The interface ID, interface version number, port vector combination is called the **interface specification**. The object UUID and location are obtained from a handle, which the calling client generates and passes as a parameter. See Chapter 9 for an explanation of handle data types and their use during remote calls.

6.5 Client Constants

Table 6-5 describes the constants used in the client FSMs.

Table 6-5. Client Constants

Name	Type	Meaning
ActivityID	UUID	The activity ID of the caller making the request.
MaxBodyLen	integer	Maximum length allowed for a single-packet *request*.
MaxPings	integer	Maximum number of unacknowledged *ping*s that should be sent in a row. The suggested value is 30.
MaxQuits	integer	Maximum number of unacknowledged *quit*s that should be sent before entering the **done** state. The suggested value is 3.
MaxRequests	integer	Maximum number of *request*s that should be sent for a single remote call. The suggested value is 5.

6.6 Client Global Variables

Table 6-6 describes the global variables used in the client FSMs.

Table 6–6. Client Global Variables

Name	Type	Meaning
bootTime	integer	The client's record of the time the server last booted.
callSpec	aggregate type	Copy of the call specification (in NDR format) from the *ClientCall* [callSpec] bundle.
idempotent	Boolean	True only if the current call is to an idempotent operation.
inFragNum	integer	The number of the last fragment of inParams sent (zero-based).
inParams	array of bytes	A copy of the input parameters (in NDR format) from the *ClientCall* [inParams] input bundle.
outFragNum	integer	The number of the last fragment of output data received in order (zero-based).
outParams	array of bytes	The reassembled (unfragmented) output data associated with the current request.
pingCount	integer	The number of consecutively sent unacknowledged *ping* packets.
quitCount	integer	The number of times a *quit* packet has been sent.
requestCount	integer	The number of times a *request* packet has been sent for the current call.
seqNum	integer	The sequence number of the current call. This value is initially 0.
waitCount	integer	The number of times the FSM has entered the **wait** state without sending a *request* packet first. The waitCount variable determines the length of time that the FSM waits in the **wait** state.

6.7 Client Primitives

Table 6–7 describes the primitives used in client FSM actions. Refer to Section 9.6 for a definition of their syntax.

Table 6–7. Client Primitives

Primitive	Meaning
RaiseException	Reflects the error that occurred in the FSM to the calling client.
SendPkt	Sets up the packet header with values specified in its input parameters and sends the data over the communications medium.
SendBroadcastPkt	Sets up the packet header with values specified in its input parameters and sends the data over the communications medium.
SendMaybePkt	Sets up the packet header with values specified in its input parameters and sends the data over the communications medium.
SendBroadcastMaybePkt	Sets up the packet header with values specified in its input parameters and sends the data over the communications medium.

6.8 Client FSM Tables

Tables 6–8 through 6–15 define the send–await–reply, broadcast, maybe, and broadcast maybe finite state machines.

Table 6-8. Send–Await–Reply FSM

State	Input	Condition	Next State	Action
init	*ClientQuit*	/	init	/
init	*ClientCall*	lengthInFrags([inParams])>1	fack_wait	*send frag request*
init	*ClientCall*	/	wait	*send request*
init	*response*	/	init	*send ack*
wait	/	requestCount>MaxRequests	done	*comm failure*
wait	*ClientQuit*	/	quit_wait	*send quit*
wait	*@WaitTimeout*	/	ping_wait	*start pinging*
wait	*fault*	/	done	*handle error*
wait	*reject*	/	done	*handle error*
wait	*working*	/	wait	*wait longer*
wait	*nocall*	/	wait	*resend request*
wait	*response*	[frag] & [fragNum] $\neq$ outFragNum+1 & [nofack]	wait	/
wait	*response*	[frag] & [fragNum] $\neq$ outFragNum+1	wait	*frag ack*
wait	*response*	[lastFrag]	done	*handle response*
wait	*response*	[frag] & [nofack]	wait	*handle frag*
wait	*response*	[frag]	wait	*handle frag; frag ack*
wait	*response*	/	done	*handle response*
ping_wait	/	pingCount>MaxPings	done	*comm failure*
ping_wait	*ClientQuit*	/	quit_wait	*send quit*
ping_wait	*working*	/	wait	*wait longer*
ping_wait	*nocall*	/	wait	*resend request*
ping_wait	*fault*	/	done	*handle error*
ping_wait	*reject*	/	done	*handle error*

(Continued)

Table 6-8. Send-Await-Reply FSM (Cont.)

State	Input	Condition	Next State	Action
ping_wait	*response*	[frag] & [fragNum] $\neq$ outFragNum+1 & [nofack]	**wait**	/
ping_wait	*response*	[frag] & [fragNum] $\neq$ outFragNum+1	**wait**	*frag ack*
ping_wait	*response*	[lastFrag]	**done**	*handle response*
ping_wait	*response*	[frag] & [nofack]	**wait**	*handle frag*
ping_wait	*response*	[frag]	**wait**	*handle frag; frag ack*
ping_wait	*response*	/	**done**	*handle response*
ping_wait	@PingWaitTimeout	/	**ping_wait**	*send ping*
fack_wait	*ClientQuit*	/	**quit_wait**	*send quit*
fack_wait	*fack*	[fragNum] $\neq$ inFragNum	**fack_wait**	*wait longer*
fack_wait	*fack*	inFragNum < lengthinFrags(inParams)	**fack_wait**	*send next frag*
fack_wait	*fack*	/	**wait**	*send last frag*
fack_wait	*nocall*	/	**fack_wait**	*resend request*
fack_wait	@FragTimeout	/	**fack_wait**	*resend request*
quit_wait	/	quitCount > MaxQuits	**done**	/
quit_wait	@QuitTimeout	/	**quit_wait**	*send quit*
quit_wait	*quack*	/	**done**	/
quit_wait	*response*	/	**done**	/
quit_wait	*nocall*	/	**done**	/
done	/	Idempotent	**init**	/
done	*ClientCall*	/	**wait**	*send request*
done	@FragTimeout	/	**done**	*send ack*

Table 6-9. Send-Await-Reply FSM Actions

send frag request
  setup request
  SendPkt(request, [frag], idempotent, seqNum, inFragNum, callSpec,
    inParams[inFragNum])

---

send request
  setup request
  SendPkt(request, [], idempotent, seqNum, 0, callSpec, inParams)

---

setup request
  seqNum ++
  idempotent := [idempotent]
  callSpec := [callSpec]
  inParams := [inParams]
  requestCount := 0
  inFragNum := 0
  outFragNum := −1
  waitCount := 0
  quitCount := 0
  requestCount := 0
  outParams := NULL

---

send ack
  SendPkt(ack, [], false, seqNum, 0, callSpec, NULL)

---

comm failure
  RaiseException(CommFailure)

---

send quit
  quitCount ++
  SendPkt(quit, [], false, seqNum, 0, callSpec, NULL)

---

start pinging
  pingCount := 0
  send ping

---

send ping
  pingCount ++
  SendPkt(ping, [], false, seqNum, 0, callSpec, NULL)

(Continued)

Table 6–9. Send–Await–Reply FSM Actions (Cont.)

---

handle error
      RaiseException(NDRtoStatus([body]))

---

wait longer
      waitCount ++

---

resend request
      requestCount ++
      waitCount := 0
      SendPkt(*request*, [], idempotent, seqNum, inFragNum, callSpec,
            inParams[inFragNum])

---

frag ack
      SendPkt(*fack*, [], false, seqNum, outFragNum, callSpec, NULL)

---

handle response
      outParams := outParams ⊕[body]
      bootTime := [bootTime]

---

handle frag
      outParams := outParams ⊕[body]
      outFragNum := [fragNum]

---

send next frag
      requestCount := 0
      waitCount := 0
      inFragNum ++
      SendPkt(*request*, [frag], idempotent, seqNum, inFragNum, callSpec,
            inParams[inFragNum])

---

send last frag
      requestCount := 0
      waitCount := 0
      inFragNum ++
      SendPkt(*request*, [frag, lastFrag], idempotent, seqNum, inFragNum,
            callSpec, inParams[inFragNum])

Table 6-10. Broadcast FSM

State	Input	Condition	Next State	Action
init	*ClientCall*	/	**wait**	*send request*
wait	@BrdcstTimeout	/	**done**	*comm failure*
wait	*fault*	/	**done**	*handle error*
wait	*reject*	/	**done**	*handle error*
wait	*response*	/	**done**	*handle response*
done	*ClientCall*	/	**wait**	*send request*
done	/	/	**init**	/

Table 6-11. Broadcast FSM Actions

```
send request
        setup request
        SendBroadcastPkt([], seqNum, 0, callSpec, inParams)


setup request
        seqNum ++
        broadcast := [broadcast]
        callSpec := [callSpec]
        inParams := [inParams]
        requestCount := 0
        outParams := NULL


comm failure
        RaiseException(CommFailure)


handle error
        RaiseException(NDRtoStatus([body]))


handle response
        outParams := outParams ⊕[body]
        bootTime := [bootTime]
```

Table 6–12. Maybe FSM

State	Input	Condition	Next State	Action
init	*ClientCall*	/	done	*send request*
done	*ClientCall*	/	done	*send request*
done	/	/	init	/

Table 6–13. Maybe FSM Actions

send request
       setup request
       SendMaybePkt([], seqNum, 0, callSpec, inParams)

---

setup request
       seqNum ++
       maybe := [maybe]
       callSpec := [callSpec]
       inParams := [inParams]
       outParams := NULL

Table 6-14. Broadcast/Maybe FSM

State	Input	Condition	Next State	Action
init	*ClientCall*	/	done	*send request*
done	*ClientCall*	/	done	*send request*
done	/	/	init	/

Table 6-15. Broadcast/Maybe FSM Actions

```
send request
        setup request
        SendBroadcastMaybePkt([], seqNum, 0, callSpec, inParams)


setup request
        seqNum ++
        broadcast := [broadcast]
        maybe := [maybe]
        callSpec := [callSpec]
        inParams := [inParams]
        outParams := NULL
```

6.9 Client Primitive Syntax Description

This section gives the syntax for the client FSM primitives.

NAME

RaiseException — Reflects an error to the client that is using the FSM.

SYNTAX

RaiseException(status)

INPUT PARAMETER

status   A reject status code (from Table 4–6).

DESCRIPTION

RaiseException is a client FSM primitive that reflects an error that occurred in the FSM to the client that is using the FSM following the error signaling conventions that the client employs.

NAME

  SendPkt — Builds an NCA/RPC packet and sends it over the communications medium.

SYNTAX

  SendPkt(*pkttype, pktflags, idempotent, seqnum, fragnum, callspec, data*)

INPUT PARAMETERS

  pkttype   A client–initiated packet type (from Table 4–1). Determines the packet type
                    field in the packet header.

  pktflags   One or more of the flags (from Table 4–2). Determines the packet flags field
                    in the packet header.

  idempotent   (Boolean) Determines whether the idempotent packet flag in the packet
                    header is set.

  seqnum   (Integer) Determines the sequence number field in the packet header.

  fragnum   (Integer) Determines the fragment number field in the packet header.

  callspec   A call specification defined in the *ClientCall* input bundle [callSpec] that
                    identifies the target interface specification, object UUID, and destination of
                    the remote call. Table 6–4 defines the values passed in [callSpec]. The values
                    in [callSpec] determine the following packet header fields:

[callSpec]	Packet Header Fields
[callSpec.if_id]	header.if_id
[callSpec.if_vers]	header.if_vers
[callSpec.opnum]	header.opnum
[callSpec.object]	header.object

                    SendPkt passes the values in *callspec* through to the destination without
                    interpretation.

  data   A variable–length string of bytes. Determines the body portion of the packet.
                    The length of *data* determines the body length field in the packet header.

DESCRIPTION

SendPkt is a client FSM primitive that sets up the packet header with values specified in its input parameters and sends the data over the communications medium to the target destination specified in [callSpec]. *SendPkt* determines the destination from [callSpec] as follows:

1. If [callSpec.location] specifies a port, *SendPkt* sends the packet to that port.

2. If [callSpec.location] specifies a port of "unspecified", *SendPkt* uses the address family specified in [callSpec.location] as an index into the port vector [callSpec.port_list] and sends the packet to the indexed port.

3. If the port in [callSpec.port_list] is "unspecified", *SendPkt* uses the LLB port specification (specified in the **port** attribute of the LLB interface definition header, defined in Chapter 11) and uses the address family specified in [callSpec.location] as an index into that list. The LLB port vector is known as the **forwarding port**.

Note that *SendPkt* only needs to use a forwarding port on the first remote call. On subsequent calls to the same destination, the client will use the port sent in the reply packet it received from the server as a *response* to the initial *request*.

NAME

SendBroadcastPkt — Builds an NCA/RPC packet and broadcasts it over the communications medium.

SYNTAX

SendBroadcastPkt(*pktflags, seqnum, fragnum, callspec, data*)

INPUT PARAMETERS

pktflags   One or more of the flags (from Table 4–2). Determines the packet flags field in the packet header. The [broadcast] packet flag is always set in broadcast *request* packets.

seqnum   (Integer) Determines the sequence number field in the packet header.

fragnum   (Integer) Determines the fragment number field in the packet header.

callspec   A call specification defined in the *ClientCall* input bundle [callSpec] that identifies the target interface specification, object UUID, and destination of the remote call. Table 6–4 defines the values passed in [callSpec]. The values in [callSpec] determine the following packet header fields:

[callSpec]	Packet Header Fields
[callSpec.if_id]	header.if_id
[callSpec.if_vers]	header.if_vers
[callSpec.opnum]	header.opnum
[callSpec.object]	header.object

SendBroadcastPkt passes the values in *callspec* through to the destination without interpretation.

data   A variable–length string of bytes. Determines the body portion of the packet. The length of *data* determines the body length field in the packet header.

DESCRIPTION

SendBroadcastPkt is a client FSM primitive that sets up the packet header with values specified in its input parameters and sends the data over the communications medium to the target destination specified in [callSpec]. *SendBroadcastPkt* determines the destination from [callSpec] in the same manner as the *SendPkt* primitive.

NAME

    SendBroadcastMaybePkt — Builds an NCA/RPC packet and sends it over the communications medium.

SYNTAX

    SendBroadcastMaybePkt (*pktflags, seqnum, fragnum, callspec, data*)

INPUT PARAMETERS

    pktflags   One or more of the flags (from Table 4–2). Determines the packet flags field in the packet header. Note that the [broadcast] and [maybe] flags are always set in maybe *request* packets.

    seqnum   (Integer) Determines the sequence number field in the packet header.

    fragnum   (Integer) Determines the fragment number field in the packet header.

    callspec   A call specification defined in the *ClientCall* input bundle [callSpec] that identifies the target interface specification, object UUID, and destination of the remote call. Table 6–4 defines the values passed in [callSpec]. The values in [callSpec] determine the following packet header fields:

[callSpec]	Packet Header Fields
[callSpec.if_id]	header.if_id
[callSpec.if_vers]	header.if_vers
[callSpec.opnum]	header.opnum
[callSpec.object]	header.object

                  SendBroadcastMaybePkt passes the values in *callspec* through to the destination without interpretation.

    data   A variable–length string of bytes. Determines the body portion of the packet. The length of *data* determines the body length field in the packet header.

DESCRIPTION

    SendBroadcastMaybePkt is a client FSM primitive that sets up the packet header with values specified in its input parameters and sends the data over the communications medium to the target destination specified in [callSpec]. *SendBroadcastMaybePkt* determines the destination from [callSpec] in the same manner as the *SendPkt* primitive.

NAME

SendMaybePkt — Builds an NCA/RPC packet and sends it over the communications medium.

SYNTAX

SendMaybePkt(*pktflags, seqnum, fragnum, callspec, data*)

INPUT PARAMETERS

pktflags   One or more of the flags (from Table 4–2). Determines the packet flags field in the packet header. Note that the [maybe] flag is always set in maybe packets.

seqnum   (Integer) Determines the sequence number field in the packet header.

fragnum   (Integer) Determines the fragment number field in the packet header.

callspec   A call specification defined in the *ClientCall* input bundle [callSpec] that identifies the target interface specification, object UUID, and destination of the remote call. Table 6–4 defines the values passed in [callSpec]. The values in [callSpec] determine the following packet header fields:

[callSpec]	Packet Header Fields
[callSpec.if_id]	header.if_id
[callSpec.if_vers]	header.if_vers
[callSpec.opnum]	header.opnum
[callSpec.object]	header.object

     SendMaybePkt passes the values in *callspec* through to the destination without interpretation.

data   A variable–length string of bytes. Determines the body portion of the packet. The length of *data* determines the body length field in the packet header.

DESCRIPTION

SendMaybePkt is a client FSM primitive that sets up the packet header with values specified in its input parameters and sends the data over the communications medium to the target destination specified in [callSpec]. *SendMaybePkt* determines the destination from [callSpec] in the same manner as the *SendPkt* primitive.

———— 🞘 ————

Chapter 7

NCA/RPC Server Protocol Specification

The NCA/RPC server protocol consists of one FSM that characterizes the server's response to a single client. The server FSM handles one client activity at a time. It does not specify how a particular client is selected; the mechanism used is implementation–dependent. Implementations of the NCA/RPC server protocol can be written to allow the server to handle multiple clients simultaneously; that is, they can choose to implement multiple instances of the server FSM's single–client handling in the same process. This chapter defines the timeouts, input data, constants, global variables, and subroutine primitives used in the server FSM table.

7.1 Server Timeouts

Table 7–1 defines the timeouts that the server FSM uses.

Table 7-1. Server Timeouts

Timeout	State	Suggested Time in State	Meaning
@ResendTimeout	**replied replying**	3 seconds	How long the server will wait for acknowledgment from the client before retransmitting a response.
@IdleTimeout	**final**	5 minutes	How long the server is required to hold information about the client activity (sequence number, activity UUID, and so on).

7.2 Execution Engine Notifications

Table 7-2 defines the notifications that the execution engine returns to the server FSM.

Table 7–2. Execution Engine Notification

Event	Meaning
CallbkCompletes	The callback that the execution engine initiated in response to a *StartCallback* call has completed. The bundle returned with this notification is [seqNum].
InvocationError	The execution engine cannot execute the operation that the *StartApplicationProcedure* primitive requested. The bundle returned with this notification is [rejectStatus].
ProcCompletes	The execution engine has executed the operation that the *StartApplicationProcedure* primitive requested. The bundle returned with this notification is [outParams].
ProcFaults	The execution engine has executed the operation that the *StartApplicationProcedure* primitive requested. The bundle returned with this notification is [faultStatus].

7.3 Execution Engine Notification Input Data

Table 7–3 defines the bundle data associated with execution engine notification input.

Table 7–3. Execution Engine Notification Input Bundles

Bundle/Notation	Type	Meaning
[faultStatus]	integer	A 32–bit fault status associated with the *ProcFaults* notification.
[outParams]	array of bytes	The output parameters (in NDR format) associated with the *ProcCompletes* notification.
[rejectStatus]	integer	A 32–bit reject status associated with the *InvocationError* notification. Reject status codes are defined in Table 4–6.
[seqNum]	integer	A 32–bit sequence number associated with the *CallbkCompletes* notification. The sequence number that represents the client's record of the current remote call.

7.4 Server Constants

Table 7–4 defines the constants used in the server FSM and actions tables.

Table 7–4. Constants

Name	Type	Meaning
BootTime	integer	A 32–bit value that indicates the time the server last booted, in UNIX time format (time in seconds since 1/1/70).
MaxBodyLen	integer	Maximum length allowed for a single–packet *response*.
MaxReplies	integer	Maximum number of times a *response* should be sent.
WrongBootTime	integer	A 32–bit value that indicates that the client's record of the server's boot time is incorrect, in UNIX time format (time in seconds since 1/1/70).

7.5 Server Global Variables

Table 7–5 defines the global variables used in server FSM and actions tables.

Table 7-5. Global Variables

Name	Type	Meaning
activityID	UUID	The universal unique identifier of the client activity that is making the remote call. This value is initially 0.
broadcast	Boolean	True only if the current call was broadcast.
fragNum	integer	The fragment number received in the packet header.
idempotent	Boolean	True only if the current call is to an idempotent procedure.
inFragNum	integer	The number of the last fragment of inParams received in order (zero-based).
inParams	array of bytes	The reassembled (unfragmented) input data associated with the current *request*.
isFrag	Boolean	True only if the frag bit in the packet flags field is set in the current *request* packet.
maybe	Boolean	True only if the current call is to a maybe procedure.
noFack	Boolean	True only if the nofack bit in the packet flags field is set in the current *request* packet.
outFragNum	integer	The number of the last fragment of output data sent (zero-based).
outParams	array of bytes	The unfragmented output data associated with the current *response*.
replyCount	integer	The number of times a reply packet has been sent for the current call.
replyType	integer	The packet type of the reply packet being returned to the client. Packet types are defined in Table 4-1.
seqNum	integer	The sequence number of the call that the server is currently processing for the client. This value is initially -1.
sourceAddress	integer	The location of the packet's sender.

7.6 Server Primitives

Table 7–6 lists the primitives used in server FSM actions.

Table 7–6. Server Primitives

Primitive	Meaning
KillApplicationProcedure	Directs the execution engine to stop the procedure, as requested by a client *quit* message.
SendPkt	Sets up the packet header with values specified in its input parameters and sends the data over the communications medium.
StartApplicationProcedure	Directs the execution engine to start the procedure requested by the client and return any output data.
StartCallback	Directs the execution engine to make a remote call to the Conversation Manager running on the machine from which the client *request* originated.

7.7 Server FSM Tables

Tables 7–7 and 7–8 define the server finite state machine.

Table 7-7. Server FSM

State	Input	Condition	Next State	Action
init	*request*	[bootTime] $\neq$ BootTime	init	*send boot time error*
init	*request*	[broadcast]	working	*do request*
init	*request*	[maybe]	working	*do request*
init	*resquest*	[frag] & [fragNum] $\neq$ 0	init	*/*
init	*request*	[frag] & [idempotent] & [nofack]	frag	*do first infrag*
init	*request*	[frag] & [idempotent]	frag	*do first infrag; frag ack*
init	*request*	[idempotent]	working	*do request*
init	*request*	/	callback	*do callback*
callback	*quit*	/	init	*send quack*
callback	*CallbkCompletes*	[seqNum] $\neq$ seqNum	init	*/*
callback	*CallbkCompletes*	isFrag & noFack	frag	*do first infrag*
callback	*CallbkCompletes*	isFrag	frag	*do first infrag;frag ack*
callback	*CallbkCompletes*	/	working	*do request*
frag	*quit*	[seqNum] $\neq$ seqNum	frag	*/*
frag	*quit*	/	final	*send quack*
frag	*request*	[frag] & [seqNum] $\neq$ seqNum	frag	*/*
frag	*request*	[frag] & [fragNum] $\neq$ inFragNum + 1	frag	*/*
frag	*request*	[frag] & [lastFrag]	working	*do request*
frag	*request*	[frag] & [nofack]	frag	*do next infrag*
frag	*request*	[frag]	frag	*do next infrag;frag ack*
working	*quit*	[seqNum] $\neq$ seqNum	working	*/*
working	*quit*	/	final	*quit call; send quack*
working	*ping*	[bootTime] $\neq$ BootTime	done	*handle error*
working	*ping*	[seqNum] > seqNum	working	*send nocall*

(Continued)

Table 7–7. Server FSM (Cont.)

State	Input	Condition	Next State	Action
working *ping*		/	**working**	*send working*
working *InvocationError*		broadcast	**init**	*free client*
working *InvocationError*		idempotent	**final**	*send reject; free reply*
working *InvocationError*		/	**replied**	*send reject*
working *ProcFaults*		idempotent	**final**	
working *ProcFaults*		/	**replied**	*send fault*
working *ProcCompletes*		maybe	**init**	*free client*
working *ProcCompletes*		lengthInFrags([outParams]) > 1	**replying**	*send first outfrag*
working *ProcCompletes*		broadcast	**final**	*send reply*
working *ProcCompletes*		idempotent	**final**	*send reply*
working *ProcCompletes*		/	**replied**	*send reply*
replying /		replyCount > MaxReplies	**final**	*free reply*
replying @ResendTimeout /			**replying**	*resend outfrag*
replying *quit*		[seqNum] = seqNum	**final**	*free reply*
replying *quit*		/	**final**	/
replying *ping*		[seqNum] = seqNum	**replying**	*send nocall*
replying *ping*		/	**replying**	*resend outfrag*
replying *fack*		[seqNum] ≠ seqNum	**replying**	/
replying *fack*		[fragNum] ≠ outFragNum	**replying**	*resend outfrag*
replying *fack*		outFragNum > lengthInFrags([outParams])	**replying**	*send next outfrag*
replying *fack*		/	**replied**	*send last outfrag*
replied /		replyCount > MaxReplies	**final**	*free reply*
replied @ResendTimeout /			**replied**	*resend reply*
replied *quit*		[seqNum] ≠ seqNum	**final**	/

(Continued)

Table 7-7. Server FSM (Cont.)

State	Input	Condition	Next State	Action
replied	*quit*	/	final	*free reply*
replied	*request*	[seqNum] $\neq$ seqNum	replied	/
replied	*request*	/	replied	/
replied	*ack*	[seqNum] $\neq$ seqNum	replied	/
replied	*ack*	/	final	*free reply*
replied	*ping*	[seqNum] > seqNum	replied	*send nocall*
replied	*ping*	/	replied	*resend reply*
final	@IdleTimeout	/	init	*free client*
final	*ping*	/	final	*send nocall*
final	*request*	[seqNum] <= seqNum	final	*send nocall*
final	*request*	[bootTime] $\neq$ BootTime	final	*send boot time error*
final	*request*	[broadcast]	working	*do request*
final	*request*	[maybe]	working	*do request*
final	*request*	[frag] & [fragNum] $\neq$ 0	final	/
final	*request*	[frag] & [nofack] & [idempotent]	frag	*do first infrag*
final	*request*	[frag] & [idempotent]	frag	*do first infrag; frag ack*
final	*request*	[idempotent]	working	*do request*
final	*request*	/	callback	*do callback*

Table 7–8. Server FSM Actions

send boot time error
          SendPkt(*reject*, [], seqNum, 0, StatustoNDR(WrongBootTime), sourceAddress)

do request
          sourceAddress := [sourceAddress]
          outParams := NULL
          outFragNum := 0
          inParams := inParams $\oplus$ [body]
          idempotent := [idempotent]
          maybe := [maybe]
          broadcast := [broadcast]
          seqNum := [seqNum]
          ifID := [ifID]
          ifVers := [ifVers]
          objectID := [objectID]
          opNum := [opNum]
          StartApplicationProcedure(ifID, ifVers, objectID, opNum, inParams)

do first infrag
          sourceAddress := [sourceAddress]
          inParams := NULL
          inParams := [body]
          seqNum := [seqNum]
          inFragNum := 0

frag ack
          SendPkt(*fack*, [], seqNum, inFragNum, NULL, sourceAddress)

do callback
          isFrag := [frag]
          noFack := [fack]
          sourceAddress := [sourceAddress]
          activityID := [activityID]
          seqNum := [seqNum]
          StartCallback(bootTime, activityID)

send quack
          inParams := NULL
          outParams := NULL
          SendPkt(*quack*, [], seqNum, 0, NULL, sourceAddress)

(Continued)

Table 7-8. Server FSM Actions (Cont.)

do next infrag
        inParams := inParams $\oplus$ [body]
        inFragNum := [fragNum]

---

quit call
        KillApplicationProcedure()
        send quack

---

send nocall
        SendPkt(nocall, [], seqNum, 0, NULL, sourceAddress)

---

send working
        SendPkt(working, [], seqNum, 0, NULL, sourceAddress)

---

free client
        This is the point at which the implementation is free to
        delete all information it is keeping about the client activity
        (activity ID, sequence number, and so on) so that it can
        optimize the amount of space available to a server that
        handles multiple clients simultaneously.

---

send reject
        outParams := StatustoNDR([rejectStatus]
        replyType := *reject*
        SendPkt(reject, [], seqNum, 0, outParams, sourceAddress)

---

free reply
        outParams := NULL

---

send fault
        outParams := StatustoNDR([faultStatus]
        replyType := *fault*
        SendPkt(fault, [], seqNum, 0, outParams, sourceAddress)

---

send first outfrag
        setup reply
        SendPkt(response, [frag], seqNum, outFragNum,
        outParams[outFragNum], sourceAddress)

(Continued)

Table 7–8. Server FSM Actions (Cont.)

---

send reply
> *setup reply*
> replyType := *response*
> SendPkt(*response*, [], seqNum, 0, outParams, sourceAddress)

---

setup reply
> outParams := [outParams]
> inFragNum := −1
> replyCount := 0

---

resend outfrag
> replyCount++
> SendPkt(*response*, [frag], seqNum, outFragNum,
>   outParams[outFragNum], sourceAddress)

---

send next outfrag
> outFragNum ++
> SendPkt(*response*, [frag], seqNum, outFragNum,
> outParams[outFragNum], sourceAddress)

---

send last outfrag
> outfragNum ++
> SendPkt (*response*, [frag, lastFrag], seqNum, outFragNum,
>   outParams[outFragNum], sourceAddress)

---

resend reply
> replyCount++
> SendPkt(replyType, [], seqNum, outFragNum,
>   outParams[outFragNum], sourceAddress)

7.8 Server Primitive Syntax Descriptions

This section defines the syntax of the primitives used in server FSM actions.

NAME

KillApplicationProcedure — Aborts execution of a remote operation.

SYNTAX

KillApplicationProcedure()

DESCRIPTION

KillApplicationProcedure is a server FSM primitive that directs the execution engine to stop executing a remote operation. The server FSM invokes this primitive in response to a client *quit* message.

NAME

> *SendPkt* — Builds an NCA/RPC packet and sends it over the communications medium.

SYNTAX

> *SendPkt(pkttype, pktflags, seqnum, fragnum, data, location)*

INPUT PARAMETERS

> *pkttype*   A server–initiated packet type (from Table 4–1). Determines the packet type field in the packet header.
>
> *pktflags*   One or more of the flags (from Table 4–2). Determines the packet flags field in the packet header.
>
> *seqnum*   (Integer) Determines the sequence number field in the packet header. This value is obtained from the [seqNum] portion of the the message input bundle to the server FSM.
>
> *fragnum*   (Integer) Determines the fragment number field in the packet header.
>
> *data*   A variable–length string of bytes. Determines the body portion of the packet. The length of *data* determines the body length field in the packet header.
>
> *location*   Socket address. Determines the destination address for the packet. This value is obtained from the [sourceAddress] portion of the message input bundle to the server FSM.

DESCRIPTION

> *SendPkt* is a server FSM primitive that sets up the packet header with values specified in its input parameters and sends the data over the communications medium to the target destination specified in the [sourceAddress] portion of the message input bundle. Note that all packet fields not modifiable by the server must retain the values established by the client FSM.

NAME

StartApplicationProcedure — Executes the operation specified in the client request.

SYNTAX

StartApplicationProcedure(interface, version, object, operation, inparams)

INPUT PARAMETERS

interface   A UUID. The universal unique identifier of the interface as specified in the *request* packet header.

version   An unsigned long integer. The version number of the interface as specified in the *request* packet header.

object   A UUID. The universal unique identifier of the object as specified in the *request* packet header.

operation   An unsigned short integer. The number of the operation within the interface as specified in the *request* packet header.

inparams   An array of bytes. The data received in the *request* body (the re-assembled data, if the client request was sent in fragments) for input to the operation.

DESCRIPTION

StartApplicationProcedure is a server FSM primitive that directs the execution engine to start the operation requested by the client and to return any output data from that operation.

NAME

   StartCallback — Starts the callback mechanism running on the server.

SYNTAX

   StartCallback(request_source, boot_time, activity)

INPUT PARAMETERS

   request_source   A socket address. The location from which the client request was sent.

   boot_time   An unsigned long integer. The time the server last booted, as specified in the global variable bootTime.

   activity   A UUID. The activity identifier contained in the *request* packet header.

DESCRIPTION

   StartCallback is a server FSM primitive that directs the execution engine to make a remote call to the **conv_$who_are_you** operation in the Conversation Manager running on the machine that generated the client request. *StartCallback* supplies the socket address given in the [sourceAddress] portion of the *request* message input bundle as *request_source*; the execution engine uses the value in *request_source* to construct a handle for input to the **conv_$who_are_you** call.

———— 🔳 ————

Chapter 8

Conversation Manager Interface

The rule for non–idempotent operations is that all non–idempotent operations are executed by the server "at most once"; that is, not at all or exactly once. The protocol that the NCA/RPC facility uses to enforce this rule is called the **callback mechanism**. The server implementation of the callback mechanism occurs in the server FSM: the protocol for non–idempotent requests requires the server to perform a callback when it receives a request from a client about which it has no information. The server makes the callback request by making a remote procedure call to the Conversation Manager at the client side; see Chapter 7 for the definition of the server callback protocol.

The Conversation Manager is the client's implementation of the callback mechanism. In addition to implementing the three FSMs defined in Chapter 6, an NCA/RPC client is required to listen for server callback requests and to implement and export the Conversation Manager interface to process them.

The Conversation Manager is an NCA–defined remote interface that processes server callback requests and returns information to the server that it uses to validate the request it has received against the client's record of its current outstanding request. The Conversation Manager runs in the calling client activity and sends the results of the callback to the socket from which the client's original request was made. The Conversation Manager is defined in an interface definition named **conv.idl**; its contents are as follows.

```
%pascal

[uuid(333a22760000.0d.00.00.80.9c.00.00.00), version(3)]

interface conv_;
import
    'nbase.idl';

[idempotent] procedure conv_$who_are_you(
                        in      h:          handle_t;
                        in ref  actuid:     uuid_$t;
                        in      boot_time:  unsigned32;
                        out     seq:        unsigned32;
                        out     st:         status_$t
                        );
end;
```

The Conversation Manager interface definition

1. Imports the interface definition file **nbase.idl,** which defines data types that the Conversation Manager requires; Appendix B gives the complete contents of **nbase.idl.**

2. Defines one idempotent operation named **conv_$who_are_you.** The next pages give syntax and usage information for **conv_$who_are_you.**

NAME

conv_$who_are_you — Implements the callback mechanism for the NCA/RPC client.

SYNOPSIS (NIDL/Pascal)

```
[idempotent] procedure conv_$who_are_you(
                    in        handle:      handle_t;
                    in ref    actuid:      uuid_$t;
                    in        boot_time:   unsigned32;
                    out       seqnum:      unsigned32;
                    out       status:      status_$t
                    );
```

DESCRIPTION

The **conv_$who_are_you** operation is an idempotent procedure that takes a calling client activity UUID and the server's record of its boot time as input, and returns the current sequence number held by the calling client and status information as output to the server making the callback.

handle	A primitive handle. See Chapter 9 for a description of primitive handles and the **handle_t** type.
actuid	The activity UUID of the calling client; in implementations that support multiple simultaneous client requests, this value is used to identify the client about whose request the server is querying.
boot_time	A 32–bit integer that identifies the time at which the server last booted. The operation stores this value in the client FSM global variable bootTime.
seqnum	A 32–bit integer that identifies sequence number associated with the client's current outstanding request.
status	Status information returned by the operation to the server that called it, in **status_$t** format; the **status_$t** type is defined in **nbase.idl**. Possible values are

YouCrashed   The server has crashed and rebooted since establishing communications with the client. The hexadecimal value for this error is defined in Table 4–6 and in the interface definition file **ncastat.idl** (Appendix C).

NotInCall   The client about whom the server is querying does not have an outstanding request in progress.

Normally, a server can detect request duplication by comparing the incoming sequence number against its record of a client's previous sequence number. However, there are three cases in which a server will have no record of a client sequence number:

- When the request is the first request from a client

- When the server has executed the request but (due to delay in client acknowledgement) has discarded all information about the client

- When the server has executed the request, but has crashed before sending the response and thus has lost all information about the client

The client and server use the *boot_time* and *seqnum* values passed between them via **conv_$who_are_you** to detect duplicate requests for non-idempotent operations in the face of acknowledgment delays or server crashes.

Acknowledgment Delays

As described in the NCA protocol summary given in Chapter 1 (and defined in the FSM tables in Chapter 7) if the server has not heard from a client for a lengthy period of time (or has run out of storage space), it discards all information about the client (that is, the response and the sequence number for that response). Consequently, when it receives a request from a client for which it has no sequence number, the server cannot determine whether the request is the first from this client, or whether it has heard from the client a long time ago and since discarded any information it formerly had about it. From the server's point of view, the received request could be a duplicate packet which it has already processed.

The server handles this case by making a remote call to the **conv_$who_are_you** operation at the calling client, passing its current boot time in *boot_time*. When it receives the callback, **conv_$who_are_you** stores the server's boot time on the client's behalf in the client FSM global variable bootTime (see Table 6-6) and sends back the client's current sequence number in *seqnum* to the server. The server compares the value of the sequence number returned in the callback to the sequence number in the client's original request. If they are identical, the server executes the original request; if not, it ignores the request. In this case, it is the server that enforces the "at most once" rule by means of the sequence number passed in the callback.

Server Crashes

A rebooted server has no sequence number about a client because it has lost all information about it as a result of the crash. Consequently, if a request arrives, the rebooted server is unable to determine whether the request is new, or whether it executed the request just before it crashed. The callback mechanism detects request duplication in this situation as follows.

1. The rebooted server must call back the client upon receipt of the request, since it will not have a sequence number.

2. The client possesses the crashed server's boot time recorded during the callback. (Since the case assumes that the crashed server has executed the call, the server must have previously called back the client.)

3. The server sends its rebooted server boot time in *boot_time* to the **conv_$who_are_you** operation. By comparing its record of the server's boot time with the value it receives in *boot_time*, **conv_$who_are_you** (or the client) can determine whether a new version of the server is calling it back. If this is so, it sends the YouCrashed error in its response to the callback. When the server receives this message, it rejects the request.

In the case of server crashes, it is the client that enforces the "at most once" rule by means of the server boot time passed in the callback.

Chapter 9

NIDL Grammar

NIDL (The Network Interface Definition Language) is the language used in NCA to describe the **remote interfaces** that clients call and servers provide. An **interface definition** written in NIDL completely defines the interface and fully specifies each remote procedure call's parameters. A NIDL remote interface provides the information needed to develop clients that use the interface's operations.

NIDL grammar is a subset of ANSI C (NIDL/C) or Pascal (NIDL/Pascal) with additional constructs to support the remote procedure call mechanism. NIDL is a declarative language; it supports C and Pascal syntax for constant, type, and operation declarations, but does not include any algorithmic structures or variables.

This chapter describes NIDL semantics and gives the syntax for NIDL/C and NIDL/Pascal grammatical constructs. Appendix A presents NIDL/C and NIDL/Pascal syntax as a collection of grammar rules formatted for input to the UNIX program **yacc**. For a description of the NCS implementation of NIDL, see the *Network Computing System Reference*.

The descriptions of NIDL/C and NIDL/Pascal grammar use a syntax notation that is similar to Extended Backus–Naur Format (EBNF); this representation of the NIDL grammar is intended to summarize the **yacc** notation in Appendix A into a readable format, and can therefore be ambiguous. Table 9–1 lists the symbols used in this format and their meaning.

Table 9-1. NIDL EBNF Format

Symbol	Meaning
::=	Is defined to be
|	Alternatively
\<text\>	Non-terminal
" "	Literal
*	The preceding syntactic unit can be repeated zero or more times
+	The preceding syntactic unit can be repeated one or more times
{}	The enclosed syntactic units are grouped as a single syntactic unit

The remainder of this chapter discusses NIDL grammar in the context of the interface definition and its structure.

9.1 Interface Definition Structure

An interface definition contains a *header* and a *body* in the following syntax:

```
C Syntax

<interface> ::= <interface_header>  "{" <interface_body> "}"
<interface_header> ::= "%c" "[" <interface_attributes>+  "]" "interface" <identifier>
<interface_body> ::= <import>* <export>+
<import> ::= "import" <import_list> ";"
<export> ::= <type_dcl> ";" | <const_dcl> ";" | <op_dcl> ";"
```

```
Pascal Syntax

<interface> ::= <interface_header> ";" <interface_body> "end;"
<interface_header> ::= "%pascal" "[" <interface_attributes>+ "]"
                        "interface" <identifier>
<interface_body> ::= <import>* <export>+
<import> ::= "import" <import_list> ";"
<export> ::= <const_def> | <type_def> | <proc_def> | <func_def>
```

9.1.1 Interface Header

The interface header consists of three elements:

- A syntax identifier that specifies the syntax of NIDL in which the interface definition is written.

- The **interface attribute list**. This list specifies the characteristics of the interface. It must be enclosed in brackets and must precede the interface name. Interface attributes are described in Section 9.2.

- The interface name. The name must be preceded by the keyword **interface**, and must be followed by an identifier that names the interface.

9.1.2 Interface Body

The interface body follows the header and can contain the following kinds of declarations:

- **Import declarations**, which specify the names of other NIDL interfaces that define data types to be used in this interface. Import declaration syntax is described in Section 9.3.

- **Constant declarations**, which specify the constants that the interface exports; constant declaration syntax is described in Section 9.4.

- **Type declarations**, which specify the type definitions that the interface exports; type declaration syntax is described in Section 9.5.

- **Operation declarations**, which specify the procedures and functions that the interface exports and the format of each, including procedure or function name, the type of data returned (if any), and the types of all parameters passed in a call to the operation. Operation declaration syntax is described in Section 9.6.

Empty interfaces (that is, interfaces that contain no declarations) are permitted.

9.2 Interface Attributes

The syntax for interface attribute declaration is

```
C Syntax
<interface_attributes> ::= < interface_attribute> { "," <interface_attribute> }*
<interface_attribute>  ::= "uuid" "(" <uuid_rep> ")"
                        | "port" "(" <port_spec> { "," <port_spec>}* ")"
                        | "implicit_handle" "(" <type_exp> <identifier> ")"
                        | "version" "(" <integer_numeric> ")"
```

```
Pascal Syntax
<interface_attributes> ::= <interface_attribute> { "," <interface_attribute> }*
<interface_attribute>  ::= "uuid" "(" <uuid_rep> ")"
                        | "version" "(" <integer_numeric> ")"
                        | "port" "(" <port_spec> { "," <port_spec> }* ")"
                        | "implicit_handle" "(" <identifier> ":" <type_exp> ")"
```

The interface attribute list must include the **uuid** attribute, which specifies the UUID for the interface. The list can also include zero or more of the following attributes, separated by commas:

- A version attribute that specifies the interface version.

- One or more port specifications that identify the well-known port or ports on which servers that export the interface will listen.

- An implicit handle global variable that specifies the handle to be used in all operations.

The interface UUID, the interface version (if any), and the port specification (if any) combination is referred to as the **interface specification**. The next sections describe the **uuid, version, port,** and **implicit_handle** attributes in more detail.

9.2.1 UUID

The **uuid** attribute designates the UUID that is assigned to the interface and which uniquely identifies it. The **uuid** attribute is expressed by the **uuid** keyword followed by a string of characters enclosed in parentheses that gives the literal representation of the UUID. This string consists of 12 hexadecimal digits followed by a period (.), followed by eight pairs of hexadecimal digits separated by periods, as shown below:

```
xxxxxxxxxxxx.ff.h1.h2.h3.h4.h5.h6.h7
```

The first 12 hexadecimal digits represent the time at which the UUID was generated. The first pair of hexadecimal digits (ff) is the protocol family; the remaining hexadecimal digit pairs give the host ID. See Chapter 2 for the complete definition of a UUID.

9.2.2 Version

The **version** attribute identifies a particular version of a remote interface. The **version** attribute is represented by the **version** keyword followed by an integer enclosed in parentheses that represents the interface version number. The version number and interface UUID combination uniquely identify a remote interface. When a client calls an operation in a remote interface, the version number and interface UUID become input to the client FSM, which passes the values in a call specification to the server FSM. See Chapter 6 for a discussion of this process.

9.2.3 Port

The **port** attribute specifies the well–known port or ports on which servers that export the interface will listen. Well–known port values are typically assigned by the central authority that "owns" the protocol. For example, the Xerox Corporation assigns well–known port values for the XNS protocol family, while the ARPANET Network Information Center assigns port values for the IP protocol family. The syntax for a port specification is

```
<port_spec> ::= <identifier> ":"  "[" <integer_numeric> "]"
```

where <identifier> specifies the name of a protocol family as defined in the **socket.h** file, and <integer_numeric> represents the well–known port within the given protocol family. The value of <integer_numeric> is a function of the protocol family specified in <identifier>; that is, the protocol family is used as an index into a vector of port numbers (see the 4.3BSD *UNIX Programmer's Manual* for a description of the **socket.h** file). Chapter 3 defines the protocol families that NCA supports.

When an application calls an operation in a remote interface, the client FSM uses the port specifications given in the interface definition to determine the location at which the call is to be delivered. See the description of the *SendPkt* client FSM primitive in Chapter 6 for an explanation of how the client FSM determines target ports for remote calls.

9.2.4 Implicit_Handle

A **handle** is an implementation–defined specification of an object's UUID and location that the NCA/RPC protocol requires to deliver a remote call to its intended destination. The object and location information contained in a handle associate, or **bind**, a remote call to an object. The client FSM uses the binding information in the handle to transmit the call request to the server that implements the operation on the particular object.

While NCA/RPC requires the presence of a handle in all remote calls, it does not specify how the binding information within it is to be defined or represented. Consequently, while a handle must contain object UUID and location information, the structure in which this information is represented is implementation–dependent. Each NCA implementation is free to design its own mechanism for binding a remote call to an object, as long as it supplies object UUID and call destination information to the client FSM protocol.

NIDL provides two methods for specifying handles:

- The **explicit handle** method, where each operation in the remote interface specifies a handle as its first parameter, and the client supplies a value for this parameter each time it calls the operation. An interface that uses explicit handles permits the caller to supply a handle value dynamically on each call to an operation.

- The **implicit handle** method, where a global variable is specified as an interface attribute that is global to all the operations in the interface. In an interface that uses implicit handles, the handle value used on calls to its operations is the value of the variable specified as the **implicit_handle** attribute; consequently, the operations do not need to define a handle parameter.

Section 9.6.3 describes how the selection of implicit or explicit handle format relates to the client FSM when an operation in a remote interface is called.

9.3 Import Declaration

The import declaration specifies an interface definition file that declares constants and data types that the importing interface uses in addition to the constants and data types that it declares itself. The import declaration is similar to the C **#include** and Pascal **%include** directives, except that it imports constant and data type names and their definitions instead of lexically including the text that defines them. The NIDL/C and NIDL/Pascal syntax for an import declaration is as follows.

```
<import> ::=  "import" <import_list> ";"

<import_list> ::= <string> { "," <string>}*
```

Each string in an import declaration identifies the pathname of an interface definition file that contains constant and data type declarations to be imported into the interface; the pathname is enclosed in single quotes.

Interface definitions can import interfaces written in either NIDL/C or NIDL/Pascal syntax. Note that an interface can only import constant and type declarations; operation declarations cannot be imported. Note also that the import declaration is idempotent; importing an interface many times has the same effect as importing it once.

9.4 Constant Declaration

The syntax for the constant declaration is

```
C Syntax

<const_dcl> ::= "const" <type_spec> <identifier> "=" <const_exp>
<const_exp> ::= <integer_literal>
              | <identifier>
              | <string_literal>
              | "nil"
              | "true"
              | "false"
```

```
Pascal Syntax

<const_defs> ::= "const" <const_def>
<const_def> ::= <identifier> "=" <const_exp> ";"
<const_exp> ::= <integer_literal>
              | <identifier>
              | <string_literal>
              | "nil"
              | "true"
              | "false"
```

A constant declaration may specify any previously defined constant as <const_exp>. In NIDL/Pascal, several constants may be declared under one **const** keyword; the declarations should be terminated by semicolons. NIDL does not currently support arithmetic constant expressions.

9.5 Type Declaration

NIDL provides constructs for naming data types; that is, it provides C and Pascal–like statements that associate an identifier with a type. NIDL/C uses the **typedef** keyword to associate a name with a data type; the syntax is

```
C Syntax

<type_dcl> ::= "typedef" <type_declarator>
<type_declarator> ::= <attributed_type_spec> <declarators>
                    |  <type_spec> <declarators>
```

NIDL/Pascal uses the **type** keyword to name a typed value; the syntax is

```
Pascal Syntax

<typedefs> ::= "type" <typedef>+
<typedef> ::= <identifier> "=" <attributed_type> ";"
```

For type declarations, NIDL defines a set of type specifiers to represent typed values and defines a set of **attributes** that can be applied to these type specifiers. The syntax is as follows.

```
C Syntax
<attributed_type_spec> ::= "[" <type_attributes> "]" <type_spec>
<type_spec> ::= <simple_type_spec> | <constructed_type_spec>
<simple_type_spec> ::= <floating_pt_type>
                     | <integer_type>
                     | <char_type>
                     | <boolean>
                     | <byte>
                     | <void>
                     | <identifier>
                     | <handle_type>

<constructed_type_spec> ::= <struct_type>
                          | <union_type>
                          | <enum_type>
                          | <set_type>
                          | <string0_type>

<declarators> ::= <declarator> { "," <declarator> }*
<declarator> ::= <simple_declarator> | <complex_declarator>
<simple_declarator> ::= <identifier>
<complex_declarator> ::=  <pointer_declarator>
                        | <array_declarator>
                        | <function_ptr_declarator>
                        | <reference_declarator>
```

```
Pascal Syntax
<attributed_type> ::= "["<type_attributes> "]" <type_exp>
<type_exp> ::= <simple_type_exp> | <structured_type_exp>
<simple_type_exp> ::= <builtin_type_exp>
                    | <enumerated_type_exp>
                    | <subrange_type_exp>
<structured_type_exp> ::= <open_array>
                        | <fixed_array>
                        | <ptr>
                        | <proc_ptr>
                        | <func_ptr>
                        | <record>
                        | <set>
                        | <string0>
```

As shown in the NIDL syntax boxes, NIDL type specifiers consist of simple C and Pascal
scalar data types and type constructors. NIDL type specifiers can be used in operation
declarations to assign data types to operation parameters. The next sections describe NIDL
type attributes and NIDL/C and NIDL/Pascal simple and constructed type specifiers.

9.5.1 Type Attributes

The following attributes can appear in a type declaration:

- **transmit_as** — permits a mapping between a presented type and a transmissible
  type

- **handle** — permits the use of user-defined, non-primitive handles

- **last_is** — allows array size to be specified dynamically

- **max_is** — allows maximum array size to be specified dynamically

The syntax for type attributes in both NIDL/C and NIDL/Pascal is

```
<type_attributes> ::= <type_attribute> { "," <type_attribute> }*

<type_attribute>  ::= "transmit_as" "(" <identifier> ")"
                    | "handle"
                    | "last_is" "(" <identifier> ")"
                    | "max_is" "(" <identifier> ")"
```

The **last_is** and **max_is** attributes can be specified in NIDL syntax as type attributes or as **field attributes** of open arrays within records (or **struct**s) or parameter lists. The **last_is** and **max_is** attributes are described in Section 9.6.2.1. The next sections describe the **transmit_as** and **handle** type attributes.

9.5.1.1 Transmit_As

The **transmit_as** attribute associates a presented type, which clients and servers manipulate, with an NDR transmissible type, which is passed in the byte stream. The implementation must provide the mechanism that converts between presented types and one of the NDR transmissible types described in Chapter 10; see the *Network Computing System Reference* for examples of mapping implementations.

A typical use of the **transmit_as** attribute is to permit operations to pass complex data types such as trees, linked lists, and records that contain pointers. In this case, the **transmit_as** attribute can be used to identify the complex type and associate it with a transmissible NDR type into which it is to be mapped; the implementation supplies the routines that perform the mapping. The **transmit_as** attribute can also be used to pass data more efficiently. For example, an implementation might provide a mechanism to convert between sparse arrays and packed arrays, sending the packed arrays over the network and presenting the sparse arrays to the application.

The **transmit_as** attribute identifies a type. Once a type is identified in this way, it can *only* be used to define a parameter; it cannot be used in any other types.

9.5.1.2 Handle

As discussed in Section 9.2.4, NCA/RPC requires that interface definitions specify handles that bind calls on their operations to the objects upon which they operate. The NIDL grammar permits handles to be specified either in the interface definition header (implicit handles) or in each operation declaration (explicit handles).

NIDL grammar also permits the definition of two types of handle: a primitive handle type and a non–primitive, user–defined handle type. A **primitive handle** contains object UUID and destination information that is meaningful to the client and server FSMs. In constrast, **non–primitive handles** permit NCA implementations to design a handle format that is meaningful to users and application programs. Non–primitive handles are identified in NIDL by the **handle** type attribute. A non–primitive handle can only be defined in a type declaration, not in an operation declaration. (See Section 9.5.2.1 for a description of primitive handles.)

Because non–primitive handles are designed for users and application programs, the binding information within them is generally not in a format that the NCA/RPC protocol recognizes. As a result, an implementation of NCA/RPC will usually require the developer of an interface definition that uses non–primitive handles to supply additional code that converts the non–primitive type to the primitive handle format required by the NCA/RPC protocol when a call is made to an operation in the interface. Section 9.6.3 describes how the choice of handle formats affects NCA/RPC protocol operation when a client makes a remote call.

9.5.2 Simple Types

The syntax for the simple types that NIDL/C and NIDL/Pascal support is as follows.

```
C Syntax

<type_spec> ::= <simple_type_spec> | <constructed_type_spec>
<simple_type_spec> ::= <floating_pt_type>
                     | <integer_type>
                     | <char_type>
                     | <boolean>
                     | <byte>
                     | <void>
                     | <identifier>
                     | <handle_type>
<floating_pt_type> ::= "float" | "double"
```

C Syntax, Continued

<integer_type> ::= <signed_int> | <unsigned_int>
<signed_int> ::= <signed_hyper_int>
          | <signed_long_int>
          | <signed_short_int>
          | <signed_small_int>

<signed_hyper_int> ::= "hyper" | "hyper" "int"
<signed_long_int> ::= "long" | "int" | "long" "int"
<signed_short_int> ::= "short" | "short" "int"
<signed_small_int> ::= "small" | "small" "int"
<unsigned_int> ::= <unsigned_hyper_int>
           | <unsigned_long_int>
           | <unsigned_short_int>
           | <unsigned_small_int>

<unsigned_hyper_int> ::= "unsigned" "hyper"
                | "hyper" "unsigned"
                | "unsigned" "hyper" "int"
                | "hyper" "unsigned" "int"

<unsigned_long_int> ::= "unsigned"
               | "unsigned" "long"
               | "long" "unsigned"
               | "unsigned" "long" "int"
               | "long" "unsigned" "int"

<unsigned_short_int> ::= "unsigned" "short"
                | "short" "unsigned"
                | "unsigned" "short" "int"
                | "short" "unsigned" "int"

<unsigned_small_int> ::= "unsigned" "small"
                | "small" "unsigned"
                | "unsigned" "small" "int"
                | "small" "unsigned" "int"

<char_type> ::= "char"
<boolean> ::= "boolean"
<byte> ::= "byte"
<void> ::= "void"
<handle_type> ::= "handle_t"

```
Pascal Syntax

<simple_type_exp> ::=   <builtin_type_exp>
                      |  <enumerated_type_exp>
                      |  <subrange_type_exp>

<builtin_type_exp> ::=   "boolean"
                      |  "char"
                      |  "integer"
                      |  "integer8"
                      |  "integer32"
                      |  "integer64"
                      |  "unsigned"
                      |  "unsigned8"
                      |  "unsigned32"
                      |  "unsigned64"
                      |  "real"
                      |  "double"
                      |  "handle_t"
                      |  <identifier>
                      |  "byte"

<enumerated_type_exp ::= "(" <identifier> { "," <identifier> }* ")"

<subrange_type_exp ::= <const_exp> ".." <const_exp>
```

The following sections discuss NIDL/C simple types and NIDL/Pascal built-in types. Section 9.5.3 discusses enumerations and subranges.

9.5.2.1 Integer Types

NIDL/C supports hyper, long, short, and small signed and unsigned integer data types. You may include the keyword **int** after any of the five other integer types; for example, **long** and **long int** are synonymous. The **int, long, unsigned,** and **unsigned long** types are represented in 32 bits. A **small** or **unsigned small** is 8 bits. A **short** or **unsigned short** is 16 bits. A **hyper** or **unsigned hyper** is 64 bits.

NIDL/Pascal supports the integer types **integer8, integer, integer32, integer64, unsigned8, unsigned, unsigned32** and **unsigned64**. The type **integer8** is represented in 8 bits. The types **integer** and **unsigned** are represented in 16 bits. An **integer32** or **unsigned32** is 32 bits. An **integer64** or **unsigned64** is 64 bits.

9.5.2.2 Floating–Point Types

NIDL/C floating–point data types are **float** and **double**. The **float** type is represented in 32 bits; the **double** type is represented in 64 bits.

NIDL/Pascal supports the floating–point types **real** (32 bits) and **double** (64 bits).

9.5.2.3 Char Type

Both NIDL/C and NIDL/Pascal define a **char** data type of eight bits.

9.5.2.4 Boolean Type (NIDL/C)

The **boolean** data type is represented in eight bits. Values for the **boolean** data type follow the Pascal convention: a value of 0 is "false," and any other value is "true."

9.5.2.5 Byte Type

The **byte** type is an 8–bit quantity that is guaranteed not to undergo any conversion when transmitted by NCA/RPC.

9.5.2.6 Void Type (NIDL/C)

The **void** data type is only used in NIDL/C; it identifies the type of function that does not return a value.

9.5.2.7 Named Type

An identifier in a type specification represents a named type declaration; that is, it identifies the name that has been assigned to a data type via the **typedef** keyword in NIDL/C or the **type** keyword in NIDL/Pascal.

9.5.2.8 Handle_t Type

As discussed in Section 9.5.1.2, NIDL permits the definition of two handle types: primitive handles and non–primitive handles. The **handle_t** type declares a variable or a parameter as a primitive handle; that is, an implementation–defined type that contains an object's UUID and location in a format that is meaningful to the client FSM. A **handle_t** type can be specified in a type declaration and in a parameter list; if it is specified in a parameter list, it must be the first parameter in the list.

The client FSM uses the information contained in the handle as input to the call specification that it builds and sends to the target destination; it also uses the location information in the handle to deliver the remote call to its intended destination. Chapter 6 describes how the client FSM builds and sends a call specification; Section 9.6.3 describes the other components of the call specification and how they are generated for input to the client FSM.

9.5.3 Constructed Types

The NIDL/C and NIDL/Pascal constructed types are

```
C Syntax
<constructed_type_spec> ::= <struct_type>
                         |    <union_type>
                         |    <enum_type>
                         |    <set_type>
                         |    <string0_type>

<complex_declarator> ::= <pointer_declarator>
                      |  <array_declarator>
                      |  <function_ptr_declarator>
                      |  <reference_declarator>
```

```
Pascal Syntax
<structured_type_exp> ::= <open_array>
                       |  <fixed_array>
                       |  <ptr>
                       |  <proc_ptr>
                       |  <func_ptr>
                       |  <record>
                       |  <set>
                       |  <string0>
```

9.5.3.1 Structures and Unions (NIDL/C)

The NIDL/C structure syntax is

```
<struct_type> ::= "struct"  "{" <member_list> "}"
<member_list> ::= <member>+
<member> ::= <attributed_type_spec> "["<field_attributes>"]" <declarators> ";"
           | <type_spec> "["<field_attributes>"]" <declarators> ";"
           | <type_spec> <declarators> ";"
<field_attributes> ::= <field_attribute> { "," <field_attribute> }*
<field_attribute> ::= "last_is" "(" <identifier> ")"
                    | "max_is" "(" <identifier> ")"
```

The **last_is** and **max_is** field attributes are described in Section 9.6.2.1.

NIDL/C does not permit structures to have tags; structure types may be named using the **typedef** statement.

Because pointers are address–space specific, **struct**s cannot contain pointers unless they are declared with the **transmit_as** attribute and the implementation–supplied conversion mechanism provides a way to de–reference them. Note that **struct**s declared with the **transmit_as** attribute are subject to the limitations described in Section 9.5.1.1 (that is, a **struct** identified with the **transmit_as** attribute can only be used to define a parameter; it can't be used in any other types).

A **struct** that contains an open array must define the array as the last member. A **struct** that contains an open array may not be returned by an operation as its value nor can it simply be an **out** parameter. The reasons for the latter restriction are discussed in Section 9.6.2.2.

The NIDL/C union syntax is

```
<union_type> ::= "union" "switch" "(" <simple_type_spec> <identifier> ")"
                       "{" <body> "}"
<body> ::= <case> { <case> }*
<case> ::= <case_label>+ <member>
<case_label> ::= "case" <const_exp> ":"
```

NIDL/C unions are a cross between the C **union** and **switch** statements. NIDL/C unions must be discriminated; that is, the union header must specify a typed tag field that determines which union member to use for the current instance of a call. NIDL/C unions limit the declarator list portion of the type declaration to one name. The **struct** restrictions on tags and pointers apply to unions as well.

9.5.3.2 Records and Variant Records (NIDL/Pascal)

The syntax for NIDL/Pascal record and variant record definitions is

```
<record> ::= "record" <record_body> "end"

<record_body> ::=  <field> { ";" <field> }* ";"
                |  <field> { ";" <field> }*
                |  <field> { ";" <field> }*  ";" <variant>
                |  <variant>

<field> ::=   "[" <field_attributes> "]"  <identifier> { "," <identifier> }*
                  ":" <attributed_type>
          |   <identifier> { "," <identifier> }*
                  ":" <attributed_type>

<field_attributes> ::= <field_attribute> { "," <field_attribute> }*

<field_attribute> ::= "last_is" "(" <identifier> ")"
                   |  "max_is" "(" <identifier> ")"

<variant> ::= "case" <identifier> ":" <type_exp> "of" <components>

<components> ::= <component>+

<component> ::=  <tag> ":" "(" <field> { ";" <field> }* ")" ";"
             |   <tag> ":" "(" <field> { ";" <field> }* ";" ")" ";"
             |   <tag> ":" "(" ")" ";"

<tag> ::= <const_exp>
```

The **last_is** and **max_is** field attributes are described in Section 9.6.2.1. Note that the restrictions on pointers and open arrays in NIDL/C structures (discussed in Sections 9.5.3.1 and 9.5.3.10) apply to NIDL/Pascal records as well.

9.5.3.3 Enumerations

Enumerated types provide names for integers. The syntax is

```
C Syntax
<enum_type> ::= { "short" | "long" } "enum" "{" <identifier> {"," <identifier>}* "}"
```

```
Pascal Syntax
<enumerated_type_exp> ::= "(" <identifier> { "," <identifier> }* ")"
```

NIDL/C defines two enumerated types: an **enum** names a 32–bit integer; a **short enum** names a 16–bit integer. NIDL/Pascal defines one enumerated type expression that names 16–bit integers. Enum identifiers are assigned integer values, beginning at 0, based on their position in the list. NIDL maps enumerated types onto the NDR integer types **unsigned short** or **unsigned long**, depending on the size of the enumerated type.

9.5.3.4 Subranges (NIDL/Pascal)

NIDL/Pascal permits the specification of a subrange of integers or of any previously defined enumeration. The syntax is

```
<subrange_type_exp> ::= <const_exp> ".." <const_exp>
```

9.5.3.5 Sets

A set is similar to an enumeration: it provides names for bits *within* single integers starting with the least significant bit of a 16–bit integer. The syntax is

```
C Syntax
<set_type> ::= "bitset" "{" <identifier> { "," <identifier> }* "}"
```

```
Pascal Syntax
<set> ::= "set" "of" <simple_type_exp>
```

NIDL maps set types onto the NDR unsigned integer types **small, short, long,** or **hyper,** depending on the size of the set.

9.5.3.6 Strings

NIDL defines the string type **string0**. A string0 is a C–style null–terminated string of a specified maximum size, including the terminating zero byte. The syntax is

```
C Syntax

<string0_type> ::= "string0" "[" <const_exp> "]"
```

```
Pascal Syntax

<string0> ::= "string0" "[" <const_exp> "]"
```

9.5.3.7 Pointers

NIDL pointers are actually **references**; that is, they are top–level pointers that point to something. NIDL provides top–level pointers to handle the C language's use of pointers as "out" parameters. A pointer declaration has the following syntax:

```
C Syntax

<pointer_declarator> ::= " * " <identifier>
```

```
Pascal Syntax

<ptr> ::= " ^ " <simple_type_exp>
```

Because NIDL pointers are references, they cannot be null. An implementation of NIDL is required to map a pointer onto the scalar or aggregate type that corresponds to the type that the pointer references. In addition, constructed types cannot contain pointers unless the **transmit_as** attribute is used and the implementation–supplied conversion mechanism provides a way to de–reference the pointer.

9.5.3.8 Function Pointers

NIDL/C defines a function pointer declaration; NIDL/Pascal defines procedure and function pointers. The syntax is

```
C Syntax

<function_ptr_declarator> ::= "(" "*" <identifier> ")" <parameter_dcls>
```

```
Pascal Syntax

<proc_ptr> ::= "^" "procedure" <parameter_list>
             | "^" "procedure"

<func_ptr> ::= "^" "function" <parameter_list> ":" <type_exp>
             | "^" "function" <parameter_list>
```

NIDL currently restricts the use of function pointers to local (that is, non–remote) interfaces. See Section 9.6 for a description of parameter list syntax.

9.5.3.9 Reference Pointer (NIDL/C)

A reference pointer consists of an identifier preceded by an ampersand. The syntax is

```
<reference_declarator> ::= "&" <identifier>
```

The reference declaration specifies that the value named by the identifier is to be passed by reference. The reference declarator is only allowed in parameter declarations, where it specifies that the parameter is to be passed by reference from the client to the server.

9.5.3.10 Arrays

NIDL defines fixed and open arrays. An **open array** is an array whose declaration does not include an explicit fixed length (that is, an array whose length will not be known until the operation in which it is used is called). Open arrays must use the **last_is** type attribute in their type declarations (the **max_is** attribute is optional). Only the first dimension of a multidimensional array can be open. NIDL/C array subscripts start at 0, while NIDL/Pascal arrays start at the index specified in the type declaration (for example, 200..400, 1..10, and so on).

An implementation of NIDL is required to map one–dimensional arrays [n..m] onto fixed arrays of size (m–n) + 1, and is required to map multidimensional arrays onto NDR one–dimensional arrays in row–major order; that is, so that the last index varies the fastest. Open multidimensional arrays must map onto NDR open one–dimensional arrays so that maximum and actual short integers are total element counts. See Chapter 10 for more information on NDR array representation.

The NIDL/C syntax for arrays is

```
C Syntax

<array_declarator> ::= <identifier> " [" "]" <fixed_array_index>*
                     | <identifier> " [" "*" "]" <fixed_array_index>*
                     | <identifier>  <fixed_array_index> +

<fixed_array_index> ::= " [" <const_exp> "]"
```

If a **struct** is to contain an open array, the array must be the last member. A **struct** that contains an open array may not be returned by an operation as its value nor can it simply be an **out** parameter. The reasons for the latter restriction are discussed in Section 9.6.2. A **union** cannot contain an open array because NDR is unable to identify which variant of the union contains the open array.

NIDL/Pascal array syntax is

```
Pascal Syntax
<open_array> ::= "array" " [" <open_indices> "]" "of" <type_exp>
<open_indices> ::= <open_index> { "," <fixed_index> }*
<open_index> ::= <const_exp> ".." "*"

<fixed_array> ::= "array" " [" <fixed_indices> "]" "of" <type_exp>
<fixed_indices> ::= <fixed_index> { "," <fixed_index> }*
<fixed_index> ::= <const_exp> ".." <const_exp>
```

The index values determine the dimensions of the array; an index value can be any simple type expression but is usually a subrange. A NIDL/Pascal open array uses an asterisk as the upper limit of the index. The restrictions on open arrays in NIDL/C **structs** also apply to NIDL/Pascal records.

9.6 Operation Declaration

Operation declarations in NIDL/C are similar to C function declarations. The syntax is

```
C Syntax

<op_dcl> ::= <routine_attributes> <simple_type_spec> <identifier> <parameter_dcls>
           | <routine_attributes>  <identifier> <parameter_dcls>
```

Operation declarations in NIDL/Pascal are similar to Pascal procedure and function declarations. The syntax is

```
Pascal Syntax

<proc_def> ::= <routine_attributes> "procedure" <identifier> <parameter_list>

<func_def ::= <routine_attributes>  "function" <identifier> ":" <type_exp> ";"
            | <routine_attributes> "function" <identifier>
              <parameter_list> ":" <type_exp> ";"
```

An operation declaration consists of

- One or more optional routine attributes that specify which protocol the client and server FSMs are to use when the operation is called. Routine attributes are described in Section 9.6.1.

- The type of the operation's function result, if any. NIDL/Pascal operations that return data must specify the data type returned. In NIDL/C, the type specifier is optional, but if it is omitted, the operation must return an **int**. For both NIDL/C and NIDL/Pascal, the type returned must be a scalar. NIDL/C operations that do not return a result must specify the **void** type in <simple_type_spec>.

- An identifier that names the operation.

- A parameter list that specifies one or more parameter declarations for the operation. Parameter declarations are optional unless the interface definition does not specify the **implicit_handle** attribute. In this case, the operation *must* define at least one parameter that specifies the explicit handle for the operation. Parameter declaration is described in Section 9.6.2.

The next sections describe routine attribute and parameter declaration syntax. Section 9.6.3 describes the meaning of a call to an operation definition in NIDL and its effect on client and server FSM functions.

9.6.1 Routine Attributes

Routine attributes specify which protocol the NCA/RPC client and server FSMs are to use. Routine attributes (also called operation attributes) are optional. The syntax for their specification is as follows:

```
<routine_attributes> ::= " [ " <routine_attribute> { " , " <routine_attribute> }* " ] "
<routine_attribute> ::= "idempotent" | "broadcast" | "maybe"
                       | <null>
```

If the operation does not specify a routine attribute, the client and server FSMs use the "at most once" protocol when the operation is called. Tables 6–8 and 6–9 define this protocol.

9.6.1.1 Idempotent Attribute

The **idempotent** keyword in an operation declaration indicates that the operation is **idempotent**: it does not modify any state and/or it yields the same result on each invocation. If an operation specifies the **idempotent** attribute, the protocol is specified by the send–await–reply client FSM; see Tables 6–8 and 6–9 for a definition of this protocol.

9.6.1.2 Broadcast Attribute

The **broadcast** keyword specifies that the NCA/RPC protocol is to broadcast the operation to all hosts on the local network each time the operation is called. When a client calls an operation with the **broadcast** attribute, the protocol is specified by the client broadcast FSM; see Tables 6–10 and 6–11 for the definition of this protocol. The output arguments that the client receives are taken from the first reply to return successfully through the client FSM; all subsequent replies are discarded. An operation with the **broadcast** attribute is implicitly an idempotent operation.

9.6.1.3 Maybe Attribute

The **maybe** keyword specifies that the operation's caller does not expect (and may not be able to handle) a response. When a client calls an operation with the **maybe** attribute, the protocol specified is the client maybe FSM, which does not guarantee delivery of the call. See Tables 6–12 and 6–13 for the definition of this protocol. An operation with the **maybe** attribute must not contain any output parameters and is implicitly an idempotent operation.

Note that an operation can specify both the **broadcast** and the **maybe** attributes; in this case, the protocol specified is the broadcast/maybe FSM defined in Tables 6-14 and 6-15.

9.6.2 Parameter Declarations

Parameter declarations in NIDL/C and NIDL/Pascal operation declarations have the following syntax:

```
C Syntax

<parameter_dcls> ::= "(" <param_dcl> { "," <param_dcl> }* ")" | "(" ")"

<param_dcl> ::=  <attributed_type_spec>  "[" <f_or_p_attributes> "]"
                         <declarator>
                  | <type_spec> "[" <f_or_p_attributes> "]"
                         <declarator>

<f_or_p_attributes> ::= <f_or_p_attribute> { "," <f_or_p_attribute> }*

<f_or_p_attribute> ::=  <field_attribute> | <param_attribute>

<field_attribute> ::= "last_is" "(" <identifier> ")"
                        | "max_is" "(" <identifier> ")"

<param_attribute> ::= "in" | "out" | "comm_status"
```

```
Pascal Syntax

<parameter_list> ::=  "(" <parameter> { ";" <parameter> }* ")"

<parameter> ::= <param_type> <identifiers> ":" <attributed_type>
                  | "[" <f_or_p_attributes> "]" <identifiers> ":" <attributed_type>

<identifiers> ::= <identifier> { "," <identifier> }*

<param_type> ::= "in" | "out" | "in out" | "in ref"

<f_or_p_attributes> ::= <f_or_p_attribute> { "," <f_or_p_attribute> }*

<f_or_p_attribute> ::=  <field_attribute> | <param_attribute>

<field_attribute> ::= "last_is" "(" <identifier> ")" | "max_is" "(" <identifier> ")"

<param_attribute> ::=  "in" | "out" | "ref" | "comm_status"
```

If the interface definition header does not specify the **implicit_handle** attribute, the first parameter in <parameter_dcls> or <parameter_list> *must* specify a handle that gives the object UUID and location. The handle can be specified as a primitive handle or as a non–primitive, user–defined handle. The meaning of handles in calls to remote operations is described in Section 9.6.3.

A parameter declaration can have attributes; NIDL defines four kinds:

- Attributes that apply to an open array parameter

- Attributes that specify the direction in which the parameter is to be passed between client and server.

- An attribute that specifies whether the parameter is passed by reference (NIDL/Pascal).

- An attribute that specifies that the parameter returns an error code in the event of a communications exception

The following sections define these attributes and give their C and Pascal syntax in parameter declarations.

9.6.2.1 Field Attributes

NIDL defines two **field attributes** which can be applied to an open array when it is defined as a field within a record (or a member of a **struct**) in a type declaration or a parameter declaration. These attributes are called **last_is** and **max_is**. The **last_is** and **max_is** attributes can appear in the record/structure or parameter declaration, as shown in the syntax boxes in Sections 9.5.3.1, 9.5.3.2, and 9.6.2. They can also be expressed syntactically as type attributes; that is, they can appear in the type attribute list, as shown in Section 9.5.1.

The **last_is** attribute allows the client and server to specify array size dynamically. It is represented by the **last_is** keyword followed by an identifier enclosed in parentheses which designates that the field or parameter named by the identifier will hold the index of the last array element to be passed. The value can be the index of the last element, which specifies that the entire array is to be passed, or it can be the index of an earlier element, which specifies that a subset of the array is to be passed. Note that the array element specified as "last" must have the same directional attributes as the open array (Section 9.6.2.2 describes NIDL directional attributes). This condition is satisfied automatically if the array and its "last" are members of the same record/structure, but must be ensured if the array and its "last" are parameters of an operation.

The **max_is** attribute allows the client to indicate the maximum possible size of an array. It is represented by the keyword **max_is** followed by an identifier, enclosed in parentheses, which designates that the field or parameter named by the identifier holds the maximum possible index of the array (note that "max" is a maximum index, not a maximum number of elements). The **max_is** attribute is typically applied to open arrays that are returned by the server (that is, to output parameters). The client assigns the value of "max," while the NIDL implementation on the server uses this information to determine how much storage to allocate for the array. Because "max" passes from client to server, it can only have the directional attributes **in** or **in out**. This rule has implications for structures that contain open arrays; Section 9.6.2.2 discusses these restrictions.

Note that open arrays do not require a **max_is** attribute. If this attribute is omitted, the implementation of NIDL can substitute the "last" variable declared for the array as if it were declared as "max." In this case, the directional requirement (**in** or **in out**) applies to "last."

The **last_is** and **max_is** identifiers must name a variable in the same scope; that is, a variable that is defined within the same structure/record or parameter list. The variable named by **last_is** and **max_is** attributes must be a scalar data type (integer or subrange).

9.6.2.2 Directional Attributes

Directional attributes inform the client and server FSMs the direction in which the parameter is to be passed. The directional attributes are:

- **in** — the parameter is passed from client to server.

- **out** — the parameter is passed from server to client.

- **in out** — the parameter is passed passed both ways.

In NIDL/C syntax, directional attributes are specified as one or more parameter attributes separated by commas and enclosed in square brackets. In NIDL/Pascal syntax, **in** and **out** can be specified either as parameter attributes or as special parameter types; **in out** can only be specified as a parameter type.

Note that a structure/record containing an open array can never simply be an **out** parameter. The reasons for this restriction are as follows:

- When a structure/record contains an open array, the **last_is** and **max_is** specifiers for the open array must be members (or fields) of the declaration.

- If a structure/record is a parameter, the directional attribute applied to the structure/record applies to all of its members.

- The **max_is** specifier (or **last_is**, if **max_is** is not used) for an open array in a parameter must have the directional attribute **in** or **in out**, since it is the client that supplies the value of **max_is** to the server.

If the array is to be passed in the **out** direction only, the structure/record must be declared with **in** and **out** directional attributes, and the client must set the field named in **last_is** to a value that causes the array segment to be empty.

9.6.2.3 Reference Attribute (NIDL/Pascal)

The reference attribute specifies that the parameter is passed by reference from the client to the server. The reference parameter attribute is a NIDL/Pascal construct; it is represented by the **in ref** keywords followed by the identifier and type. In NIDL/C, a parameter to be passed by reference is defined as a reference declarator (see Section 9.5.3.9).

9.6.2.4 Communications Status Attribute

The **comm_status** attribute designates that the parameter will hold an error code in the event that the operation incurs a communications exception during remote execution. It is the responsibility of the NIDL implementation to catch the exception and generate the error code to be returned in the parameter.

9.6.3 Semantics of a Call to an Operation in a Remote Interface

When a client calls a remote operation, the NCA/RPC client FSM constructs a call specification that describes the target interface, operation, and object upon which the operation is to be performed. The call specification contains the following values:

- The UUID and version of the interface that contains the operation being called

- The UUID of the object on which the operation is to be performed

- The number of the operation being called

- The location to which the call is to be delivered

- The values supplied for the **in** arguments (if any) defined for the operation

This information is determined outside the client FSM by the calling client, the interface definition, and the operation declaration, as follows:

1. The interface definition that contains the operation being called determines the interface UUID and version; the values used in the call specification are those supplied as interface and version attributes in the interface header.

2. The handle supplied in the remote call determines the object UUID and location information; the steps taken to pass the handle information to the client FSM depend upon the kind of handle defined for the operation, as follows:

    - If the called operation specifies a primitive **handle_t** type as its first parameter, the UUID and location information used in the call specification come directly from the handle parameter passed by the client. NIDL syntax for primitive handles is described in Section 9.5.2.8.

- If the called operation specifies a non–primitive, user–defined handle type as its first parameter, the conversion mechanism for the handle type must be invoked to map the non–primitive handle to the primitive **handle_t** type. The UUID and location information used in the call specification are the converted values. NIDL syntax for non–primitive handle types is described in Section 9.5.1.2.

- If the called operation does not specify a handle parameter at all, the interface in which it is defined uses implicit handles rather than explicitly specifying them as operation parameters. In this case, the object UUID and location information used in the call specification is derived from the handle global variable that is defined with the **implicit_handle** attribute in the interface definition header. If this handle is a non–primitive type, the conversion mechanism must be invoked; otherwise, the client FSM takes the UUID and location information directly from the implicit handle. Note that handle–less operations can *only* exist if the interface definition specifies an implicit handle. NIDL syntax for implicit handle specification is described in Section 9.2.4.

3. The position of the operation within the list of operations in the interface determines the operation number.

4. The calling client supplies values to parameters defined in the operation definition. Values for parameters marked with the **in** directional attribute are converted to an NDR byte stream for input to the client FSM. When the client FSM builds the packet, these values become the contents of the request packet body. When the call completes at the server side, parameters marked with the **out** attribute are converted to an NDR byte stream for input to the server FSM. These values become the contents of the response packet body.

———— 🔡 ————

Chapter 10

Network Data Representation

NIDL is a language for describing procedures to be called remotely via the NCA/RPC protocol (as described in Chapter 9). While a NIDL interface specifies abstract typed values, the NCA/RPC protocol expects a byte stream as input to the client FSM. NDR provides a way to describe a NIDL–defined sequence of typed values in a byte stream by defining a set of transmissible scalar data types and aggregate type constructors. When an application program calls a remote interface, the implementation of NIDL uses the set of transmissible types that NDR defines to map the input parameters specified in the call to values in a byte stream; the result is a mapping between an ordered set of typed values and a byte stream.

NDR also defines a set of representation formats and a **format label** that identifies the particular data representation format being used to represent scalar values in the byte stream; the format is established dynamically when an application makes a remote procedure call. The set of formats and the format label represents NDR's multicanonical approach to data conversion between machines (described in Chapter 1).

This chapter describes

- The set of NDR transmissible scalar types and the supported data representation formats for these types

- The set of NDR aggregate type constructors

- The structure of the format label

10.1 NDR Transmissible Types and Their Representations

The set of transmissible scalars consists of **boolean**, **character**, **signed** and **unsigned integer** (4 sizes), **floating-point** (2 sizes), and **byte** data types. All data types are multiples of bytes in length; a byte is eight bits. NDR requires scalar values to be **naturally aligned** in the byte stream. Under natural alignment, all scalar values of size 2^n are aligned at a byte stream index that is a multiple of 2^n, up to some limiting value of n; NDR defines this limit to be 3.

10.1.1 Boolean

The data type **boolean** represents a logical quantity that can assume one of two values: **true** or **false**. NDR represents a boolean in the byte stream as one byte. It represents a value of **false** as a 0 byte, and represents a value of **true** as a nonzero byte. Figure 10-1 illustrates the boolean data type as it appears in the byte stream.

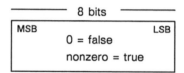

Figure 10-1. Boolean Data Type

10.1.2 Character

NDR represents a character in the byte stream as a single byte. Characters have two representation formats: **ASCII** and **EBCDIC**. Appendix D provides an ASCII/EBCDIC conversion chart. Figure 10-2 illustrates the character type as it appears in the byte stream.

Figure 10-2. Character Data Type

10.1.3 Integer

NDR supports both **signed** and **unsigned** (non–negative) integers, and defines four sizes for both types:

- **small** — An 8–bit integer (represented in the byte stream as one byte)

- **short** — A 16–bit integer (represented in the byte stream as two bytes)

- **long** — A 32–bit integer (represented in the byte stream as four bytes)

- **hyper** — A 64–bit integer (represented in the byte stream as eight bytes)

NDR represents signed integers in two's complement notation and represents unsigned integers as unsigned binary numbers. Integers have two formats: **big–endian** and **little–endian**. If the integer format is big–endian, the bytes of the representation are ordered in consecutive bytes of the byte stream from most–significant byte (MSB) to least–significant byte (LSB). If the integer format is little–endian, the bytes of the representation are ordered in consecutive bytes of the byte stream from least–significant byte to most–significant byte. Figure 10–3 illustrates the integer types in big–endian and little–endian format.

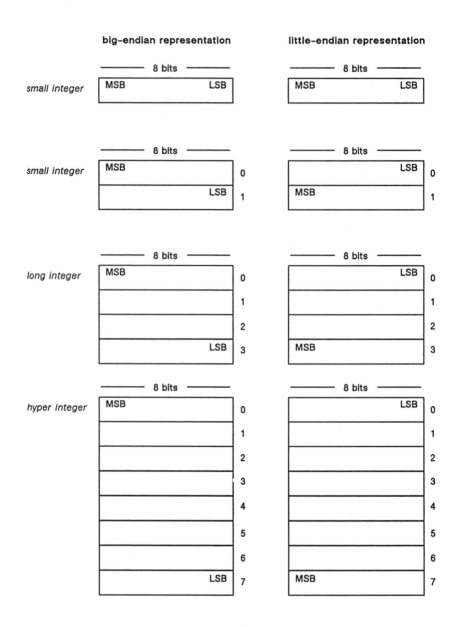

Figure 10–3. Big–Endian and Little–Endian Integer Formats

10.1.4 Floating–Point Types

NDR defines the floating–point types **single precision** and **double precision**; it represents single–precision floating–point numbers as four bytes in the byte stream, and represents double precision as eight bytes. NDR supports the following floating–point data representation formats for single-precision and double-precision floating point:

- IEEE single and double floating point, which comply with IEEE standard 754.

- VAX F_floating and G_floating formats as defined in the *VAX11 Architecture Handbook*, Copyright 1979, Digital Equipment Corporation.

- Cray floating–point format, as defined in the documentation produced by Cray Research, Inc.

- IBM short and long formats, as defined in the *IBM System/370 Principles of Operation*, Copyright 1974, International Business Machines Corporation.

Table 10–1 is a conversion chart for NDR single– and double–precision floating–point types and the supported floating–point formats.

Table 10–1. NDR Floating–Point Conversions

NDR Values	Conversion Values			
	IEEE	VAX	Cray	IBM
single	single (4 bytes)	F (4 bytes)	single (4 bytes)	short (4 bytes)
double	double (8 bytes)	G (8 bytes)	double (8 bytes)	long (8 bytes)

Floating–point numbers consist of three fields:

- The **sign** field, which indicates the sign of the number; values 0 and 1 represent positive and negative, respectively. This field is one bit in length.

- The **exponent** of the number, base 16 for IBM format, base 2 for all others. The size of this field varies depending on the floating–point format in use.

- The fractional part of the number's mantissa, base 16 for IBM, base 2 for all others. (This field is also called the number's **coefficient**.) The size of the fraction varies according to the floating–point format in use.

The next subsections illustrate how floating–point numbers are represented in the byte stream according to IEEE, VAX, Cray, and IBM formats.

10.1.4.1 IEEE Format

If the format label specifies IEEE format, NDR uses IEEE single representation to represent single–precision floating–point values, and uses IEEE double representation to represent double–precision floating–point values. Single IEEE floating–point format is 32 bits in length, consisting of a 1–bit sign, an 8–bit exponent field (excess 127) and a 23–bit mantissa that represents a fraction in the range 1.0 (inclusive) to 2.0 (exclusive). Double IEEE floating–point format is 64 bits in length with a 1–bit sign, an 11–bit exponent (excess 1023), and a 52–bit mantissa.

IEEE floating–point numbers can be generated on machines made by different manufacturers and with different architectures. Some of these machines (for example, 80x86 machines) use little–endian integer representation, while other machines (for example, M680x0 machines) use big–endian integer representation. Bytes of floating–point numbers sent from a machine using little–endian integer format are in reverse order from bytes sent from a machine that uses big–endian format. Consequently, when a recipient interprets an NDR byte stream tagged in the format label as using IEEE floating–point format, it uses the integer representation in the format label to determine the byte order of the IEEE floating–point number. Figures 10–4 and 10–5 illustrates IEEE single–precision and double–precision floating–point format in big–endian and little–endian integer representation.

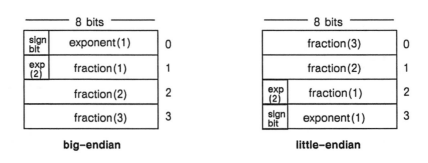

Figure 10–4. IEEE Single–Precision Floating–Point Format

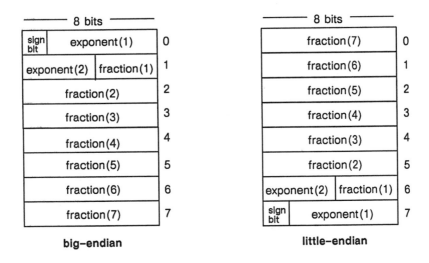

Figure 10–5. IEEE Double–Precision Floating–Point Format

10.1.4.2 VAX Format

The VAX architecture defines four floating–point types: F_floating, D_floating, G_floating, and H_floating. F_floating format is 32 bits in length, including a 1–bit sign, an 8–bit exponent (excess 128), and a 23–bit mantissa that represents a fraction in the range 0.5 (inclusive) to 1.0 (exclusive). D_floating format is 64 bits with a 1–bit sign, an 8–bit exponent, and a 56–bit mantissa. G_floating format is also 64 bits, with a 1–bit sign, an 11–bit exponent (excess 1024), and a 52–bit mantissa. H_floating is 128 bits.

Although the VAX architecture supports four kinds of floating–point formats, NDR uses only the VAX F_floating format to represent VAX single–precision floating–point numbers, and uses the VAX G_floating format to represent VAX double–precision floating–point numbers. Figures 10–6 and 10–7 illustrate VAX F and G floating–point representations as they appear in the byte stream.

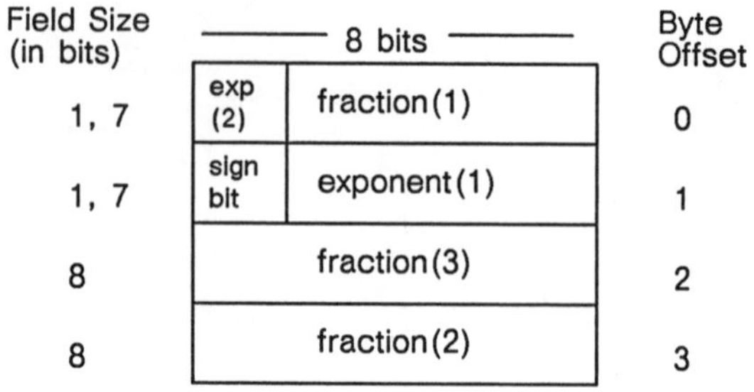

Field Size (in bits)	——— 8 bits ———	Byte Offset
1, 7	exp (2) | fraction(1)	0
1, 7	sign bit | exponent(1)	1
8	fraction(3)	2
8	fraction(2)	3

Figure 10-6. VAX Single-Precision (F) Floating-Point Format

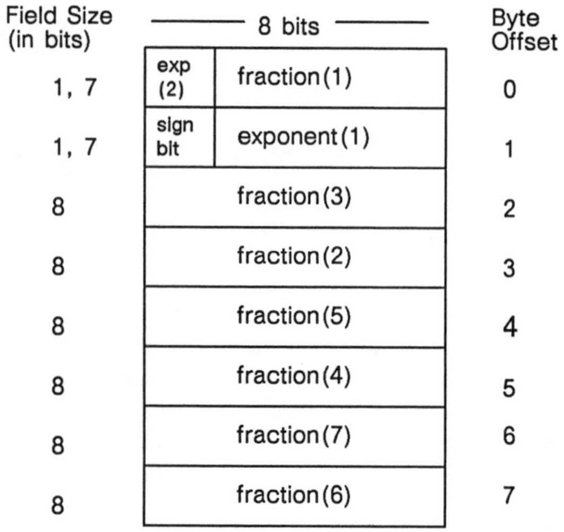

Field Size (in bits)	——— 8 bits ———	Byte Offset
1, 7	exp (2) | fraction(1)	0
1, 7	sign bit | exponent(1)	1
8	fraction(3)	2
8	fraction(2)	3
8	fraction(5)	4
8	fraction(4)	5
8	fraction(7)	6
8	fraction(6)	7

Figure 10-7. VAX Double-Precision (G) Floating-Point Format

Table 10-2 defines the fields in Figure 10-6 in VAX architecture terms.

Table 10-2. VAX F Floating-Point Fields

Field Name	Bit Field
Exponent(1)	8:14
Exponent(2)	7:7
Sign Bit	15:15
Fraction(1)	0:6
Fraction(2)	24:31
Fraction(3)	16:23

Figures 10-6 and 10-7 illustrate VAX F and G floating-point format as they appear on VAX machines, which use a little-endian format for integer representation. However, some machines may implement VAX floating-point format but use big-endian integer format to represent integers. Consequently, a recipient interpreting an NDR byte stream tagged in the format label as using VAX floating-point format must use the integer representation in the format label to determine the byte order of the floating-point number.

10.1.4.3 Cray Format

Cray machine architecture defines only a double-precision floating-point format. A Cray double-precision floating-point number is 64 bits in length and consists of a 1-bit sign, a 15-bit exponent (16384 excess) and a 48-bit fraction. However, because Cray machines may be required to handle single-precision floating-point values (because a remote interface specifies single-precision values in the interface definition), NDR defines a single-precision floating-point format for the Cray.

A Cray single-precision floating-point number is identical to IEEE format: it is 32 bits in length and consists of a 1-bit sign, an 8-bit exponent, (excess 127), and a 23-bit mantissa that represents a fraction in the range 1.0 (inclusive) to 2.0 (exclusive). Figure 10-8 illustrates the Cray floating-point formats.

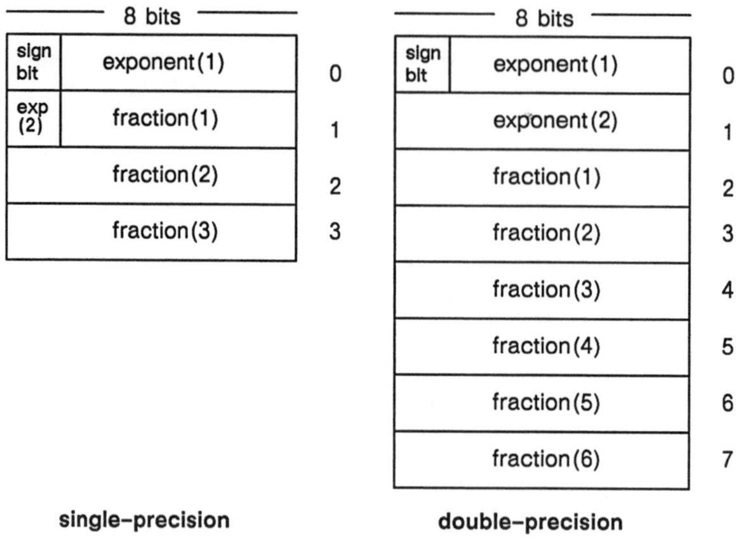

Figure 10-8. Cray Floating-Point Formats

10.1.4.4 IBM Format

The IBM architecture defines single-precision and double-precision floating-point values using its short and long floating-point formats, respectively. IBM short floating-point numbers consist of a 1-bit sign, a 7-bit exponent, and a 24-bit fraction. IBM long floating-point numbers consist of a 1-bit sign, a 7-bit exponent, and a 56-bit fraction. IBM represents both the exponent and fraction in hexadecimal notation rather than in binary. Consequently, the exponent is base 16, while the fraction is composed of six 4-bit hexadecimal digits or fourteen 4-bit hexadecimal digits. Figure 10-9 illustrates the IBM short and long floating-point formats.

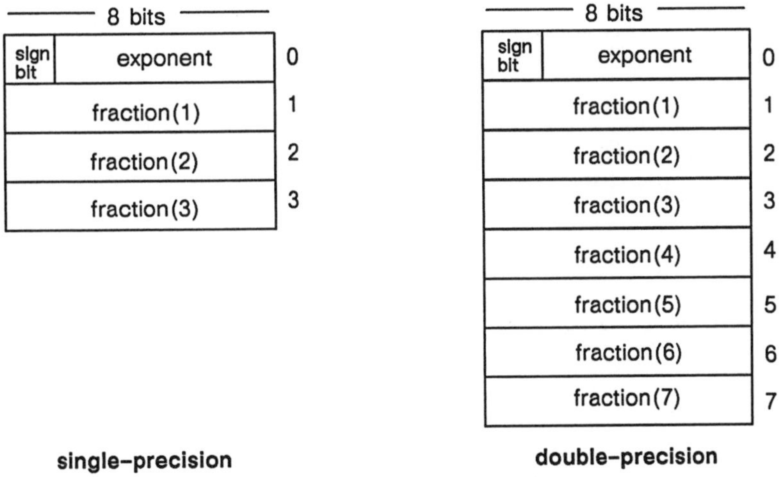

single-precision   **double-precision**

Figure 10–9. IBM Floating–Point Format

Figure 10–9 illustrates IBM floating–point format as it appears on IBM 360 machines, which use a big–endian integer representation. However, some machines may implement IBM floating–point with a little–endian integer representation. Consequently, when a recipient interprets an NDR byte stream tagged in the format label as using IBM floating–point format, it must use the integer representation in the format label to determine the byte order of the floating–point number. Note also that IBM PCs use the IEEE single–precision format, rather than the IBM short format.

10.1.5 Byte

NDR represents the **byte** type as an uninterpreted byte; that is, no conversions are made on **byte** type data. NDR also allows the definition of arrays of uninterpreted bytes.

10.2 Constructed and Aggregate Types

In addition to scalar types, NDR defines **fixed array**, **open array**, **varying array**, **record**, **variant record**, and **open record** constructed types and defines the aggregate type **zero-terminated string**.

10.2.1 Fixed Arrays

A **fixed array** represents an ordered, one–dimensional, homogeneous, indexed collection of values whose type and number of elements are specified in the array type definition. The elements of an array may be any element type (scalar, constructed, or aggregate). The elements themselves may also be arrays; however, they may not be open arrays. Because NDR recognizes only one–dimensional arrays, the NIDL implementation is responsible for transforming multi–dimensional arrays into single–dimensional arrays. NDR does not permit an open array or an open record to be an array element.

NDR represents a fixed array in the byte stream as an ordered sequence of element representations; it represents each element value according to the array's element type. Figure 10–10 illustrates a fixed array as it appears in the byte stream; the ellipsis indicates the existence of elements between the first and last elements. Note that there may be gaps between elements due to natural alignment of element values; this is not shown in the figure.

Figure 10–10. Fixed Array Representation

10.2.2 Open Arrays

An **open array** represents an ordered, one–dimensional, homogeneous collection of data whose type is specified in the array type definition, but whose maximum and actual number of elements varies. The elements of an open array may be any element type (scalar, constructed, or aggregate). NDR currently limits the size of open arrays to 65535 (2^16–1) elements.

NDR represents an open array in the byte stream by the representation of its maximum number of elements (an unsigned short integer), followed by the representation of its actual number of elements (an unsigned short integer), followed by the representations of each element value. The maximum element value appears first in the representation because the array's recipient may need to use it to determine the amount of storage it must allocate to hold the array elements. The maximum and actual values in the NDR open array representation correspond to values supplied for the **max_is** and **last_is** attributes defined in the NIDL open array declaration. See Section 9.6.2.1 for more information about **last_is** and **max_is** attributes and their use.

Figure 10–11 illustrates the representation of an open array; the ellipsis indicates the existence of elements between the first and last element representations. Note that an open array representation is even–byte aligned because of the unsigned short integer that appears at the beginning of the representation. A 2–, 4–, or 6–byte gap may exist between the representation of the actual number of elements and the representation of the first element in the array; the size of the gap depends on the element type's alignment requirements. In addition, there may be gaps between elements due to natural alignment of element values; neither of these possible gaps are shown in the figure.

2 bytes	2 bytes	size per element type		size per element type
maximum number of pos-sible elements	actual number of elements = n	1st element representation	• • •	nth element representation

Figure 10–11. Open Array Representation

10.2.3 Varying Arrays

A **varying array** represents an ordered, one–dimensional, homogeneous collection of data whose type and maximum number of elements are specified in the array type definition, but whose actual number of elements varies. An NDR varying array corresponds to a NIDL array that is declared to be a fixed size, but whose actual size is modified with the **last_is** attribute. NDR represents a varying array by the representation of its actual number of elements (an unsigned short integer), followed by the representations of each element value. The actual number of elements in the NDR varying array representation corresponds to the value supplied for the **last_is** attribute used with the NIDL varying array.

Figure 10–12 illustrates the varying array as encoded in the byte stream; the ellipsis indicates the existence of elements between the first and last elements. A gap may exist between the representation of the actual number of elements and the representation of the first element in the array; the size of the gap depends on the element type's alignment requirements. In addition, there may be gaps between elements due to natural alignment of element values; neither of these possible gaps are shown in the figure.

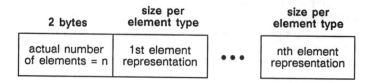

Figure 10-12. Varying Array Representation

10.2.4 Records

A **record** represents an ordered, possibly heterogeneous collection of data whose types and number are specified in the record type definition. A record field may be of any type, either scalar or constructed, except for open arrays or open records. NDR represents a record in a byte stream by the representations of its fields in the order in which the record defines them. The field's type determines the number of bytes required to encode it.

Figure 10-13 illustrates the record type as encoded in the byte stream; the ellipsis indicates the existence of elements between the first and last fields. Note that there may also be gaps in fields due to natural alignment of field values; this is not shown in the figure.

Figure 10-13. Record Type Representation

10.2.5 Variant Records

A **variant record** represents an ordered, possibly heterogeneous collection of data whose types and number are specified in the record definition, but whose actual fields and number vary. NDR specifies that variant records have an initial set of fixed fields, including a **tag** field used to discriminate among the possible variants. The NDR representation of a variant record in a byte stream consists of the representations of its fixed field values followed by the representations of the selected variant's fields. The tag field can occur at any position within the fixed-field representations; however, in NIDL definitions, it generally appears last.

Figure 10-14 illustrates a variant record as it appears in the byte stream; the ellipsis indicates the existence of elements between the first and last field representations. Note that there may also be gaps due to natural alignment of field values; this is not shown in the figure.

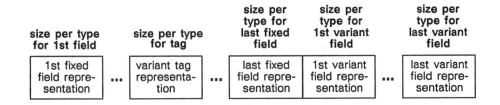

Figure 10–14. Variant Record Representation

10.2.6 Open Records

An **open record** is a nonvariant record whose last field is either an open array or another open record. NDR represents an open record by the representation of the maximum number of array elements in the ending open array field (an unsigned short), followed by the representations of the record's fixed–length fields, followed by the representation of the actual number of open array elements (an unsigned short integer), followed by the representations of the open array elements. The maximum number of open array elements appears first because the recipient may need to use this value to determine how much storage to allocate for the open record. The actual number of elements is not used for storage allocation determination and therefore does not need to be placed before the record representation.

Figure 10–15 illustrates an open record as it appears in the byte stream; the ellipsis indicates the series of field representations. An open record is even–byte aligned because of the unsigned short integer that appears at the beginning of the representation. Note that there may also be gaps due to natural alignment of field and element values; this is not shown in the figure.

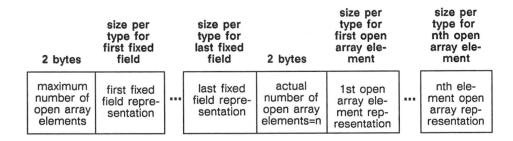

Figure 10–15. Open Record Representation

10.2.7 Zero–Terminated Strings

A **zero–terminated string** can be viewed as a special kind of open array: it is an open array of characters whose last element is a 0 byte. NDR represents a zero–terminated string as the number of characters in the string (an unsigned short integer), followed by the string's characters according to the format (ASCII or EBCDIC) specified in the format label, followed by a terminating 0 byte. The number of characters in the string appears first in the representation because the string's recipient uses the value to determine the amount of storage it must allocate to hold the string. The presence of this unsigned short integer means that a zero–terminated string representation is even–byte aligned.

Figure 10–16 illustrates the representation of a zero–terminated string as it appears in the byte stream.

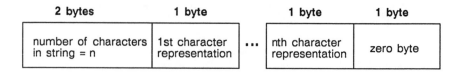

Figure 10–16. Zero–Terminated String Representation

10.3 Data Representation Format Label

The NDR format label is a vector of bytes that identifies the particular data representation format being used to represent scalar values in the byte stream so that machines with differing formats can communicate with each other via the multicanonical conversion protocol described in Chapter 1. Figure 10–17 illustrates the NDR format label. Integer representation occupies the four most–significant bits (MSB) of the first byte, character representation occupies the four least–significant bits (LSB) of the first byte; floating–point representation occupies the second byte, while the third and fourth bytes are reserved for future use and must contain 0s.

```
        MSB ───────── 8 bits ───────── LSB
       ┌──────────────────┬──────────────────┐
byte 1 │     integer      │    character     │
       │  representation  │  representation  │
       ├──────────────────┴──────────────────┤
byte 2 │      floating-point representation  │
       ├─────────────────────────────────────┤
byte 3 │        reserved for future use      │
       ├─────────────────────────────────────┤
byte 4 │        reserved for future use      │
       └─────────────────────────────────────┘
```

Figure 10-17. Data Representation Format Label

Table 10-3 shows the values associated with integer, character, and floating-point formats. Integer, character, and floating-point formats are established dynamically when an application makes a remote procedure call; the values associated with these formats are registered in the format label at this time.

Table 10-3. Format Label Values

Data Type	Value in Label	Format
character	0	ASCII
	1	EBCDIC
integer	0	big-endian
	1	little-endian
floating-point	0	IEEE
	1	VAX
	2	Cray
	3	IBM

Chapter 11

NCA/LB Specification

A highly available location service is a fundamental component of a distributed system architecture. Objects (which represent people, resources, or services) are transient, mobile entities in a network environment. Consumers of these entities cannot rely on a priori knowledge of their existence or location. Instead, they must be able to determine these entities' existence or location dynamically by consulting a location service.

The NCA/LB is NCA's mechanism for providing clients with information about the locations of objects and interfaces. Object, object type, and interface information is contained in a database; an NCA/LB protocol provides access to this database.

Servers register their location and the objects, types of objects, and interfaces they support in the NCA/LB database. They specify their location by using socket addresses, and identify the objects, types, and interfaces they support by listing their UUIDs in the database entry.

Clients query about objects, object types, and interfaces by specifying their UUIDs in remote calls to the NCA/LB. When presented with a UUID, the NCA/LB returns the socket address of a server that has registered that it handles the object, object type, or interface associated with that UUID.

The NCA/LB is organized into **Global Location Broker (GLB)** and **Local Location Broker (LLB)** components. The GLB maintains information about objects and interfaces throughout the network; it consists of a GLB database and a protocol that controls access to this database. Implementations of the GLB protocol can choose to replicate the GLB database object to ensure that global location information remains available despite a partial network failure. NCA does not currently specify a replication protocol, nor does it specify a protocol for maintaining consistency among GLB replicas.

The LLB maintains information about objects and interfaces located at the local host; it consists of an LLB database and a protocol that controls access to this database. The LLB supports servers that wish to limit their registration to the local system. A client can directly query an LLB at a specific system to determine the objects and servers that are registered there.

The GLB and LLB protocols are specified in two separate interfaces. The GLB is defined in an interface definition file named **glb.idl**; its contents are as follows.

```
{ Global Location Broker Interface }

%pascal
[uuid(333b2e690000.0d.00.00.87.84.00.00.00),version(4)]
interface glb_;
import
        'nbase.idl';
const
        lb_$mod                 = 16#1C020000;
        lb_$database_invalid    = 16#1C020001;

        lb_$database_busy       = 16#1C020002;
        lb_$not_registered      = 16#1C020003;

        lb_$update_failed       = 16#1C020004;
        lb_$cant_access         = 16#1C020005;
        lb_$server_unavailable  = 16#1C020006;

type
        lb_$server_flag_t = integer32;

const
        lb_$server_flag_local         = 16#00001;
        lb_$server_flag_reserved_02   = 16#00002;
        lb_$server_flag_reserved_04   = 16#00004;
        lb_$server_flag_reserved_08   = 16#00008;
        lb_$server_flag_reserved_10   = 16#00010;
        lb_$server_flag_reserved_20   = 16#00020;
        lb_$server_flag_reserved_40   = 16#00040;
        lb_$server_flag_reserved_80   = 16#00080;
        lb_$server_flag_reserved_0100 = 16#00100;
        lb_$server_flag_reserved_0200 = 16#00200;
        lb_$server_flag_reserved_0400 = 16#00400;
        lb_$server_flag_reserved_0800 = 16#00800;
        lb_$server_flag_reserved_1000 = 16#01000;
        lb_$server_flag_reserved_2000 = 16#02000;
        lb_$server_flag_reserved_4000 = 16#04000;
        lb_$server_flag_reserved_8000 = 16#08000;
        lb_$server_flag_reserved_10000 = 16#10000;
        lb_$server_flag_reserved_20000 = 16#20000;
        lb_$server_flag_reserved_40000 = 16#40000;
        lb_$server_flag_reserved_80000 = 16#80000;
```

```
type
        lb_$lookup_handle_t = integer32;
const
        lb_$default_lookup_handle = 0;
type
        lb_$entry_t = record
        {* uuid_$nil == wildcard in each of the object_spec fields *}
                object          : uuid_$t;
                obj_type        : uuid_$t;
                obj_interface   : uuid_$t;
                flags           : lb_$server_flag_t;
                annotation      : array [0..63] of char;
                saddr_len       : integer32;
                saddr           : socket_$addr_t;
                end;

{* glb_$insert - add the specified entry to the global database.*}

procedure
    glb_$insert (
        in        h        : handle_t;
        in ref    entry    : lb_$entry_t;
        out       status   : status_$t
    );

{* glb_$delete - remove the specified entry from the global database.*}

procedure
    glb_$delete (
        in        h        : handle_t;
        in ref    entry    : lb_$entry_t;
        out       status   : status_$t
    );

{* glb_$lookup - perform a lookup operation on the global database.*}

[ idempotent ] procedure
    glb_$lookup (
        in        h               : handle_t;
        in ref    object          : uuid_$t;
        in ref    obj_type        : uuid_$t;
        in ref    obj_interface    : uuid_$t;
        in out    entry_handle    : lb_$lookup_handle_t;
        in        max_num_results : integer32;
        out       num_results     : integer32;
        out       result_entries  : [ last_is(num_results),
                                            max_is(max_num_results) ]
                                        array [ 1..* ] of lb_$entry_t;
        out       status          : status_$t
    );
```

```
{* glb_$find_server - the LB implementation uses this routine to find a
   Global Location Broker that is in service. It is normally implemented
   as an empty routine.*}

[ broadcast ] procedure
   glb_$find_server (
        in      h        : handle_t
   );
end;
```

The LLB is defined in an interface definition file named **llb.idl**; its contents are as follows.

```
{ Local Location Broker Interface }

%pascal
[uuid(333b33c30000.0d.00.00.87.84.00.00.00),
 port(dds:[12],ip:[135]),
 version(4)]
interface llb_;
import
        'nbase.idl',
        'glb.idl';

{* llb_$insert - add the specified entry to the database.*}

procedure
    llb_$insert (
        in      h        : handle_t;
        in ref  entry    : lb_$entry_t;
        out     status   : status_$t
    );


{* llb_$delete - remove the specified entry from the database.*}

procedure
    llb_$delete (
        in      h        : handle_t;
        in ref  entry    : lb_$entry_t;
        out     status   : status_$t
    );
```

```
{* llb_$lookup - perform a lookup operation at a local database.*}

[ idempotent ] procedure
    llb_$lookup (
        in      h               : handle_t;
        in ref  object          : uuid_$t;
        in ref  obj_type        : uuid_$t;
        in ref  obj_interface    : uuid_$t;
        in out  entry_handle     : lb_$lookup_handle_t;
        in      max_num_results  : integer32;
        out     num_results      : integer32;
        out     result_entries   : [ last_is(num_results),
                                      max_is(max_num_results) ]
                                      array [ 1..* ] of lb_$entry_t;
        out     status           : status_$t
    );
end;
```

The GLB interface definition

1. Imports the interface definition file **nbase.idl,** which defines NCA base data types that the GLB network interface requires; Appendix B gives the contents of **nbase.idl.**

2. Defines a set of types and constants for both the GLB and LLB network interfaces. Sections 11.1 and 11.2 give usage information about these definitions.

3. Defines the following operations:

   - **glb_$insert** — a non–idempotent operation that adds an entry to the global database

   - **glb_$delete** — a non–idempotent operation that removes an entry from the global database

   - **glb_$lookup** — an idempotent operation that searches the global database

   - **glb_$find_server** — a broadcast operation that finds a Global Location Broker server

   Section 11.3 gives usage information about GLB operations.

The LLB interface definition

1. Imports the interface definition file **nbase.idl,** which defines NCA base data types that the LLB network interface requires. Appendix B gives the contents of **nbase.idl.**

2. Imports the **glb.idl** interface definition file, which defines LB data types that the LLB network interface requires.

3. Gives an LLB port specification at which servers exporting the LLB interface are to listen. This port specification consists of the well-known port number 12 for the DDS protocol family (assigned by Apollo) and 135 for the Internet protocol family (assigned by DARPA). Chapter 3 describes protocol families and well-known ports in more detail, while Chapter 9 defines how to represent port specifications in NIDL syntax.

4. Defines the following operations (which are semantically identical to their GLB counterparts):

   - **llb_$insert** — a non-idempotent operation that adds an entry to the local database

   - **llb_$delete** — a non-idempotent operation that removes an entry from the local database

   - **llb_$lookup** — an idempotent operation that searches the local database

Note that a server listening on the LLB well-known port should provide the forwarding mechanism described in the client FSM *SendPkt* primitive. See Section 6.9 for information about this primitive.

The remainder of this chapter describes the NCA/LB types, constants, and error values, and gives syntax and usage information for GLB and LLB operations.

11.1 NCA/LB Data Types and Constants

A common set of types and constants is defined for both GLB and LLB protocols; the sets are defined in the GLB interface (**glb.idl**) and imported by the LLB interface (**llb.idl**). Tables 11–1 and 11–2 describe the NCA/LB constants and data types, respectively. The bit layout of the NCA/LB data types is determined by the NDR protocol's representation of the data type and by the local data representation format. See Chapter 10 for an explanation of NDR data type representation and format.

Table 11–1. NCA/LB Constants

Constant	Meaning
lb_$server_flag_local	Used in the flags field of an **lb_$entry_t** data type to indicate that the server that implements the interface is available to the local node only and should be registered only in the LLB database. This constant is assigned the value 1.
lb_$default_lookup_handle	Used as a value for the **lb_$lookup_handle_t** type when it is an input parameter to the LLB/GLB lookup operation, directing the operation to begin the lookup at the start of the LLB/GLB database. This constant is assigned the value 0.

Table 11-2. NCA/LB Data Types

Data Type	Meaning
lb_$entry_t	A record that identifies an object, type, interface, socket address tuple used to access a server that exports the interface to the object. Table 11-3 describes the fields of an **lb_$entry_t** type.
lb_$lookup_handle_t	An unsigned long integer used to specify the location in the LLB/GLB database at which an LLB/GLB lookup operation is to start. The constant **lb_$default_lookup_handle** assigned to this type directs the LLB/GLB to begin searching at the beginning of the database.
lb_$server_flag_t	An unsigned long integer that defines bit flags used in LLB/GLB protocol control.
	Bit 0 Controls where an **lb_$entry_t** appears. When set, the entry should appear in the LLB database. When clear, the entry should appear in both LLB and GLB databases. The bit set value is defined to be the constant **lb_$server_flag_local**.
	Bits 1-31 Reserved for future use.

Table 11–3. The lb_$entry_t Fields

Field	Meaning
object	The UUID for the object. NCA defines a **uuid_$nil** value that can be assigned to this field; when present, it indicates that there is no object associated with the interface. The Conversation Manager is an example of an interface that has no object associated with it.
object type	The UUID for the type associated with the object. NCA defines a **uuid_$nil** value that can be assigned to this field; when present, it indicates that the object has no type associated with it.
interface	The UUID for the interface. NCA defines a **uuid_$nil** value that can be assigned to this field; when present, it indicates that there is no interface associated with the entry.
flags	Must be 0 or **lb_$server_flag_local**.
annotation	An array of characters that stores a textual description of the object and interface for informational purposes. The maximum number of characters permitted in this field is 64.
socket address length	An unsigned long integer that gives the length of the socket address field. This length is equal to the number of meaningful bytes in the data field of the socket address plus two bytes.
socket address	A socket address, in **socket_$addr_t** format, that uniquely identifies the location of the server. The **socket_$addr_t** data type is defined in **nbase.idl** (see Appendix B); Chapter 3 gives a description of its use.

11.2 NCA/LB Error Codes

The GLB and LLB interfaces use a common set of error codes shown in Table 11–4. These error codes are defined as constants in **glb.idl** and imported by **llb.idl**.

Table 11–4. NCA/LB Error Codes

Status	Value	Meaning
lb_$database_invalid	1C020001	The format of the LB database is out of date. The database may have been created by an old version of the LLB/GLB, or the LLB or GLB that accessed it may be running out-of-date software.
lb_$database_busy	1C020002	The requested LLB/GLB database cannot be opened.
lb_$not_registered	1C020003	The LLB/GLB cannot find an entry that matches the criteria specified in the lookup or delete operation.
lb_$update_failed	1C020004	The LLB/GLB was unable to complete the insert or delete operation.
lb_$cant_access	1C020005	The LLB/GLB cannot access the LLB/GLB database.
lb_$server_unavailable	1C020006	The requested LLB or GLB server cannot be reached, either because of a communications failure or because the server is not running.

11.3 GLB and LLB Operations

The next pages give syntax and usage information for GLB and LLB operations.

NAME

glb_$insert — Adds an entry to the Global Location Broker database.

SYNTAX (NIDL/Pascal)

```
procedure glb_$insert (
                in          handle:      handle_t;
                in ref      xentry:      lb_$entry_t;
                out         status:      status_$t
                );
```

DESCRIPTION

The **glb_$insert** operation is the first operation defined in the GLB interface. It is a non-idempotent operation that adds an entry to the GLB database. The **glb_$insert** operation replaces an existing entry with the specified new entry if the object UUID, object type UUID, interface UUID, and protocol family and host in the socket address field match the existing entry. Otherwise, it creates a new entry. Subsequent lookup calls will return the inserted entry.

handle   A primitive handle that identifies the target GLB object and server for the insert operation. See Chapter 9 for a description of primitive handles and the **handle_t** data type.

xentry   An **lb_$entry_t** type. The entry to be added to the GLB database. The entry contains a unique combination of object UUID, object type UUID, interface UUID, and socket address.

status   Status information returned by the operation to its caller, in **status_$t** format; **status_$t** format is defined in **nbase.idl**, shown in Appendix B. Table 11–4 lists the set of error codes to be returned in this parameter. Possible values returned by **glb_$insert** are:

lb_$database invalid
The format of the GLB database is out of date. The database may have been created by an old version of the GLB, or the GLB that accessed it may be running out-of-date software.

lb_$database busy
The GLB was unable to open the GLB database.

lb_$update_failed

> The GLB was unable to complete the insert operation.

lb_$cant_access

> The GLB cannot access the GLB database.

lb_$server_unavailable

> The requested GLB server cannot be reached, either because of a communications failure or because the server is not running.

NAME

glb_$delete — Deletes an entry from the Global Location Broker database.

SYNTAX (NIDL/Pascal)

procedure glb_$delete (
in	*handle*:	**handle_t;**
in ref	*xentry*:	**lb_$entry_t;**
out	*status*:	**status_$t**

);

DESCRIPTION

The **glb_$delete** operation is the second operation in the GLB interface definition. It is a non–idempotent procedure that searches the GLB database for the entry that matches the contents of the specified entry and deletes it. The object UUID, object type UUID, interface UUID, and socket address value (with the exception of the port field) specified in the call must all match a given entry before **glb_$delete** will remove the entry. Note that you cannot use **uuid_$nil** as a wildcard for deleting entries. The value **uuid_$nil** is not a valid value to supply to **glb_$delete** unless the intent is to delete an entry that actually contains a **uuid_$nil** value.

handle   A primitive handle that identifies the target GLB object and server for the delete operation. See Chapter 9 for a description of primitive handles and the **handle_t** data type.

xentry   An **lb_$entry_t** type. The entry to be removed from the database.

status   Status information returned by the operation to its caller, in **status_$t** format; the **status_$t** data type is defined in **nbase.idl**. Table 11–4 lists the set of error codes to be returned in this parameter. Possible values returned by **glb_$delete** are:

lb_$database invalid
    The format of the GLB database is out of date. The database may have been created by an old version of the GLB, or the GLB server that accessed it may be running out-of-date software.

lb_$database busy
    The GLB was unable to open the GLB database.

lb_$not registered
    The GLB server cannot find an entry that matches the criteria specified in the **glb_$delete** call.

lb_$cant_access

> The GLB cannot access the GLB database.

lb_$server_unavailable

> The requested GLB server cannot be reached, either because of a communications failure or because the server is not running.

NAME

glb_$lookup — Looks up information in the Global Location Broker database.

SYNTAX (NIDL/Pascal)

```
[idempotent] procedure glb_$lookup (
    in          handle:         handle_t;
    in ref      object:         uuid_$t;
    in ref      obj_type:       uuid_$t;
    in ref      obj_interface:  uuid_$t;
    in out      entry_handle:   lb_$lookup_handle_t;
    in          max_results:    integer32;
    out         num_results:    integer32;
    out         result_entries: [last_is(num_results),  max_is(max_results)]
                                    array [1..*] of lb_$entry_t;
    out         status:         status_$t
    );
```

DESCRIPTION

The **glb_$lookup** procedure is the third operation in the GLB interface. The operation returns GLB entries that contain matching object UUID, type UUID, and interface UUID identifiers. The value **uuid_$nil** in any of these parameters acts as a wildcard and will match all values in the corresponding entry field.

handle	A primitive **handle_t** type that identifies the target GLB object and server for the lookup operation. See Chapter 9 for a description of primitive handles and the **handle_t** data type.
object	A **uuid_$t** type. The UUID of the object to look up.
obj_type	A **uuid_$t** type. The UUID of the type to look up.
obj_interface	A **uuid_$t** type. The UUID of the interface to look up.
entry_handle	An **lb_$lookup_handle_t** type. A location in the database.

As an input parameter, the *entry_handle* specifies the location in the GLB database to start the lookup. The **lb_$default_lookup_handle** constant in this parameter directs the operation to start the lookup at the beginning of the database.

As a return value, the *entry_handle* specifies the next unsearched part of the GLB database; that is, the point at which the next search should begin. The constant **lb_$default_lookup_handle** as a return value indicates that the search found at most *max_results* matching entries before it reached the end of the database.

max_results   An unsigned long integer. The maximum number of matching entries that can be returned by a single lookup operation. This value should be the same as the number of elements in the *result_entries* array.

num_results   An unsigned long integer. The number of GLB entries returned by the operation.

result_entries   An array of **lb_$entry_t** type. This array contains the matching database entries, up to the number specified in the *max_results* parameter. If the array contains any entries for servers on the local network, those entries appear first.

status   Status information returned by the operation to its caller, in **status_$t** format; the **status_$t** type is defined in **nbase.idl**, shown in Appendix B. Table 11–4 lists the set of error codes to be returned in this parameter. Possible values returned by **glb_$lookup** are:

lb_$database invalid
> The format of the GLB database is out of date. The database may have been created by an old version of the GLB, or the GLB server that accessed it may be running out-of-date software.

lb_$database busy
> The GLB was unable to open the GLB database.

lb_$not registered
> The GLB server cannot find an entry that matches the criteria specified in the **glb_$lookup** call.

lb_$update_failed
> The GLB server was unable to complete the delete operation.

lb_$cant_access
> The GLB server cannot access the GLB database.

lb_$server_unavailable
> The requested GLB server cannot be reached, either because of a communications failure or because the server is not running.

The lookup operation cannot return more than *max_results* matching entries at a time. The input parameter *entry_handle* provides the ability to perform sequential lookup operations to find all matching entries in the GLB database. However, if multiple lookup operations are issued to find all matching results, the returned information may skip or duplicate entries from the database. This is because the GLB protocol does not prevent modification of the database between lookups, and such modifications can change the locations of entries relative to an *entry_handle* value.

NAME

glb_$find_server — Locates a Global Location Broker server.

SYNTAX (NIDL/Pascal)

[broadcast] procedure glb_$find_server (
    in   *handle*:   **handle_t**
    );

DESCRIPTION

The **glb_$find_server** operation is the fourth operation in the GLB interface. It locates a GLB server by broadcasting a message to the LLB well-known port.

handle   A primitive **handle_t** type that specifies the LLB well-known port (defined in **llb.idl**). See Chapter 9 for a description of primitive handles and the **handle_t** format; see Chapter 3 for an explanation of well-known ports.

Successful completion of **glb_$find_server** causes *handle* to be bound to the GLB server that responded to the broadcast; subsequent calls that use this *handle* will be directed to this server.

NAME

llb_$insert — Adds an entry to the Local Location Broker database.

SYNTAX (NIDL/Pascal)

procedure llb_$insert (

in	*handle*:	**handle_t;**
in ref	*xentry*:	**lb_$entry_t;**
out	*status*:	**status_$t**
);		

DESCRIPTION

The **llb_$insert** operation is the first operation defined in the LLB interface definition. It
is a non–idempotent operation that adds an entry to the LLB database. The **llb_$insert**
operation replaces an existing entry with the specified new entry if the object UUID, object
type UUID, interface UUID, and protocol family and host in the socket address field
match the existing entry. Otherwise, it creates a new entry. Subsequent lookup calls will
return the inserted entry.

handle   A primitive **handle_t** type that identifies the target LLB object and server
                for the insert operation. See Chapter 9 for a description of primitive han-
                dles and the **handle_t** data type.

xentry   An **lb_$entry_t** type. The entry to be added to the LLB database. The
                entry contains a unique combination of object UUID, object type UUID,
                interface UUID, and socket address.

status   Status information returned by the operation to its caller, in **status_$t**
                format; the **status_$t** type is defined in **nbase.idl**, shown in Appendix B.
                Table 11–4 lists the set of error codes to be returned in this parameter.
                Possible values returned by **llb_$insert** are:

lb_$database invalid
                The format of the LLB database is out of date. The database
                may have been created by an old version of the LLB, or the
                LLB that accessed it may be running out-of-date software.

lb_$database busy
                The LLB was unable to open the LLB database.

lb_$update_failed
                The LLB was unable to complete the insert operation.

lb_$cant_access
>The LLB cannot access the LLB database.

lb_$server_unavailable
>The requested LLB server cannot be reached, either because of a communications failure or because the server is not running.

NAME

llb_$delete — Deletes an entry from the Local Location Broker database.

SYNTAX (NIDL/Pascal)

procedure llb_$delete (
                    in   *handle*:   handle_t;
                    in ref   *xentry*:   lb_$entry_t;
                    out   *status*:   status_$t
                    );

DESCRIPTION

The **llb_$delete** operation is the second operation defined in the LLB interface. It is a non–idempotent procedure that searches the LLB database for the entry that matches the contents of the specified entry and deletes it. Note that you cannot use **uuid_$nil** as a wildcard for deleting entries. The value **uuid_$nil** is not a valid value to supply to **llb_$delete** unless the intent is to delete an entry that actually contains a **uuid_$nil** value. The object UUID, object type UUID, interface UUID, and socket address value (with the exception of the port field) specified in the call must all match a given entry before **llb_$delete** will remove the entry.

handle   A primitive **handle_t** type that identifies the target LLB object and server for the delete operation. See Chapter 9 for a description of primitive handles and the **handle_t** data type.

xentry   An **lb_$entry_t** type. The entry to be removed from the database.

status   Status information returned by the operation to its caller, in **status_$t** format; the **status_$t** data type is defined in **nbase.idl**, shown in Appendix B. Table 11–4 lists the set of error codes to be returned in this parameter. Possible values returned by **llb_$delete** are:

                  lb_$database invalid
                          The format of the LLB database is out of date. The database may have been created by an old version of the LLB, or the LLB server that accessed it may be running out–of–date software.

                  lb_$database busy
                          The LLB was unable to open the LLB database.

                  lb_$not registered
                          The LLB server cannot find an entry that matches the criteria specified in the **llb_$delete** call.

lb_$cant_access
> The LLB cannot access the GLB database.

lb_$server_unavailable
> The requested LLB server cannot be reached, either because of a communications failure or because the server is not running.

NAME

llb_$lookup — Looks up information in the Local Location Broker database.

SYNTAX (NIDL/Pascal)

```
[idempotent] procedure llb_$lookup (
    in          handle:         handle_t;
    in ref      object:         uuid_$t;
    in ref      obj_type:       uuid_$t;
    in ref      obj_interface:  uuid_$t;
    in out      entry_handle:   lb_$lookup_handle_t;
    in          max_results:    integer32;
    out         num_results:    integer32;
    out         result_entries: [last_is(num_results), max_is(max_results)]
                                    array [1..*] of lb_$entry_t;
    out         status:         status_$t
    );
```

DESCRIPTION

The **llb_$lookup** operation is the third operation defined in the LLB interface. It returns LLB entries that contain matching object UUID, type UUID, and interface UUID identifiers. The value **uuid_$nil** in any of these parameters acts as a wildcard and will match all values in the corresponding entry field.

handle   A primitive handle that identifies the target LLB object and server for the lookup operation. See Chapter 9 for a description of primitive handles and the **handle_t** data type.

object   A **uuid_$t** type. The UUID of the object to look up.

obj_type   A **uuid_$t** type. The UUID of the type to look up.

obj_interface   A **uuid_$t** type. The UUID of the interface to look up.

entry_handle   An **lb_$lookup_handle_t** type. A location in the database.

As an input parameter, the *entry_handle* specifies the location in the LLB database to start the lookup. The **lb_$default_lookup_handle** constant in this parameter directs the operation to start the lookup at the beginning of the database.

As a return value, the *entry_handle* specifies the next unsearched part of the LLB database; that is, the point at which the next search should begin. The constant **lb_$default_lookup_handle** as a return value indicates that the search found at most *max_results* matching entries before it reached the end of the database.

max_results	An unsigned long integer. The maximum number of matching entries that can be returned by a single lookup operation. This value should be the same as the number of elements in the *result_entries* array.
num_results	An unsigned long integer. The number of LLB entries returned by the operation.
result_entries	An array of **lb_$entry_t** type. This array contains the matching database entries, up to the number specified in the *max_results* parameter. If the array contains any entries for servers on the local network, those entries appear first.
status	Status information returned by the operation to its caller, in **status_$t** format; the **status_$t** type is defined in **nbase.idl,** shown in Appendix B. Table 11–4 lists the set of error codes to be returned in this parameter. Possible values returned by **llb_$lookup** are:

lb_$database invalid

    The format of the LLB database is out of date. The database may have been created by an old version of the LLB, or the LLB server that accessed it may be running out–of–date software.

lb_$database busy

    The LLB was unable to open the LLB database.

lb_$not registered

    The LLB server cannot find an entry that matches the criteria specified in the **glb_$lookup** call.

lb_$update_failed

    The LLB server was unable to complete the delete operation.

lb_$cant_access

    The LLB server cannot access the LLB database.

lb_$server_unavailable

    The requested LLB server cannot be reached, either because of a communications failure or because the server is not running.

The lookup operation cannot return more than *max_results* matching entries at a time. The input parameter *entry_handle* provides the ability to perform sequential lookup operations to find all matching entries in the LLB database. However, if multiple lookup operations are issued to find all matching results, the returned information may skip or duplicate entries from the database. This is because the LLB protocol does not prevent modification of the database between lookups, and such modifications can change the locations of entries relative to an *entry_handle* value.

Appendix A

NIDL yacc Input Specification

The **yacc** input file for NIDL consists of a declaration section that defines the NIDL tokens (a **token** is an entity that cannot be further decomposed, such as a number or an identifier) and a rules section that gives the grammar rules for NIDL/Pascal and NIDL/C. Each **yacc** rule references a token or another **yacc** rule. Representing the NIDL grammar as a **yacc** input file produces an unambiguous specification of NIDL/Pascal and NIDL/C and allows the specification to be used as input to **yacc** to generate NIDL/C and NIDL/Pascal parsers. The NIDL specification given in this appendix follows the conventions and notation for **yacc** input file generation. See the 4.3BSD *UNIX Programmer's Supplementary Documents, Volume 1* for a complete description of these conventions.

The **yacc** input on the pages that follow gives NIDL keywords, common NIDL syntax, NIDL/Pascal–specific syntax, and NIDL/C–specific syntax, respectively. Note that the printed representations of keywords are case insensitive in NIDL/Pascal and case sensitive in NIDL/C.

```
%{

%token  ARRAY_KW
%token  BITSET_KW
%token  BOOLEAN_KW
%token  BYTE_KW
%token  CHAR_KW
%token  CASE_KW
%token  COMM_STATUS_KW
%token  CONST_KW
%token  DOUBLE_KW
%token  END_KW
%token  FROM_KW
%token  FUNCTION_KW
%token  IDEMPOTENT_KW
%token  IN_KW
```

```
%token IMPLICIT_HANDLE_KW
%token IMPORT_KW
%token INCLUDE_KW
%token INTEGER_KW
%token INTEGER8_KW
%token INTEGER32_KW
%token INTEGER64_KW
%token INTERFACE_KW
%token LAST_IS_KW
%token MAYBE_KW
%token MAX_IS_KW
%token NIL_KW
%token OF_KW
%token OTHERWISE_KW
%token OUT_KW
%token PORT_KW
%token PROCEDURE_KW
%token RECORD_KW
%token REAL_KW
%token REMOTE_KW
%token SET_KW
%token STRING0_KW
%token TAG_IS_KW
%token TYPE_KW
%token UUID_KW
%token UNION_KW
%token UNSIGNED_KW
%token UNSIGNED8_KW
%token UNSIGNED32_KW
%token UNSIGNED64_KW
%token VERSION_KW
%token HYPER_KW
%token LONG_KW
%token SHORT_KW
%token FLOAT_KW
%token VOID_KW
%token SMALL_KW
%token SWITCH_KW
%token TYPEDEF_KW
%token STRUCT_KW
%token ENUM_KW
%token INT_KW
%token REF_KW
%token OPTION_KW
%token HANDLE_T_KW
%token HANDLE_KW
%token UUID_REP
%token TRANSMIT_AS_KW
%token TRUE_KW
%token FALSE_KW
%token BROADCAST_KW
%token UNIV_PTR_KW
```

```
%token COLON
%token COMMA
%token DOTDOT
%token EQUAL
%token HAT
%token LBRACE
%token LBRACKET
%token LPAREN
%token RBRACE
%token RBRACKET
%token RPAREN
%token SEMI
%token STAR
%token AMPER
%token IDENTIFIER
%token STRING
%token INTEGER_NUMERIC

%start interface
%%
interface:
        interface_attributes INTERFACE_KW IDENTIFIER interface_tail
    ;
interface_tail:
        pascal_interface_tail
    |   c_interface_tail
    ;
pascal_interface_tail:
        pas_interface_marker interface_body pas_interface_close
    ;
pas_interface_marker:
        SEMI
    ;
pas_interface_close:
        END_KW SEMI
    ;
interface_attributes:
        attribute_opener interface_attr_list attribute_closer
    |   /* Nothing */
    ;
attribute_opener:
        LBRACKET
    ;
attribute_closer:
        RBRACKET
    ;

interface_attr_list:
        interface_attr
    |   interface_attr_list COMMA interface_attr
    ;
```

```
interface_attr:
        IMPLICIT_HANDLE_KW LPAREN IDENTIFIER COLON
            builtin_type_exp RPAREN
    |   IMPLICIT_HANDLE_KW LPAREN c_simple_type_spec IDENTIFIER   RPAREN
    |   UUID_KW UUID_REP
    |   PORT_KW LPAREN port_list RPAREN
    |   VERSION_KW LPAREN INTEGER_NUMERIC RPAREN
    ;

port_list:
        port_spec
    |   port_list COMMA port_spec
    ;
port_spec:
        IDENTIFIER COLON LBRACKET INTEGER_NUMERIC RBRACKET
    ;
interface_body:
        exports
    |   imports exports
    |   /* nothing */
    ;
imports:
        import
    |   imports import
    ;
import:
        IMPORT_KW import_list SEMI
    ;
import_list:
        import
    |   import_list COMMA import
    ;
import:
        STRING
    ;
exports:
        export
    |   exports export
    ;

export:
        CONST_KW const_defs
    |   TYPE_KW  type_defs
    |   proc_def
    |   func_def
    ;

const_defs:
        const_def
    |   const_defs const_def
    ;
const_def:
```

```
            IDENTIFIER EQUAL const_exp   SEMI
      ;
const_exp:
            INTEGER_NUMERIC
      |     IDENTIFIER
      |     STRING
      |     NIL_KW
      |     TRUE_KW
      |     FALSE_KW
      ;


type_defs:
            type_def
      |     type_defs type_def
      ;
type_def:
            IDENTIFIER EQUAL attributed_type SEMI
      ;
attributed_type:
            type_attribute_list   type_exp
      |     type_exp
      ;
type_attribute_list:
            attribute_opener type_attributes attribute_closer
      ;
type_attributes:
            type_attribute
      |     type_attributes COMMA type_attribute
      ;
type_attribute:
            LAST_IS_KW LPAREN IDENTIFIER RPAREN
      |     MAX_IS_KW LPAREN IDENTIFIER RPAREN
      |     HANDLE_KW
      |     TRANSMIT_AS_KW LPAREN IDENTIFIER RPAREN
      ;
type_exp:
          simple_type_exp
      |   structured_type_exp
      ;
simple_type_exp:
            builtin_type_exp
      |     enumerated_type_exp
      |     subrange_type_exp
      ;


builtin_type_exp:
          BOOLEAN_KW
      |   BYTE_KW
      |   CHAR_KW
      |   INTEGER_KW
      |   INTEGER8_KW
```

```
        |   INTEGER32_KW
        |   INTEGER64_KW
        |   UNSIGNED_KW
        |   UNSIGNED8_KW
        |   UNSIGNED32_KW
        |   UNSIGNED64_KW
        |   REAL_KW
        |   DOUBLE_KW
        |   HANDLE_T_KW
        |   IDENTIFIER
        |   UNIV_PTR_KW
        ;
enumerated_type_exp:
        |   LPAREN enum_ids RPAREN
        ;
enum_ids:
            enum_id
        |   enum_ids COMMA enum_id
        ;
enum_id:
            IDENTIFIER
        ;
subrange_type_exp:
            const_exp DOTDOT const_exp
        ;
structured_type_exp:
            open_array_type_exp
        |   fixed_array_type_exp
        |   ptr_type_exp
        |   record_type_exp
        |   set_type_exp
        |   proc_ptr_type_exp
        |   func_ptr_type_exp
        |   string0_type_exp
        ;

open_array_type_exp:
            ARRAY_KW LBRACKET open_array_index RBRACKET OF_KW type_exp
        |   ARRAY_KW LBRACKET open_array_index COMMA fixed_array_indices
                RBRACKET OF_KW type_exp
        ;
fixed_array_type_exp:
            ARRAY_KW LBRACKET fixed_array_indices RBRACKET OF_KW type_exp
        ;

open_array_index:
            const_exp DOTDOT STAR
        ;
fixed_array_indices:
            fixed_array_index
        |   fixed_array_indices COMMA fixed_array_index
        ;
```

```
fixed_array_index:
        simple_type_exp
    ;
ptr_type_exp:
        HAT simple_type_exp
    ;
set_type_exp:
        SET_KW OF_KW simple_type_exp
    ;
record_type_exp:
        RECORD_KW record_body END_KW
    ;
record_body:
        field_specs
    |   field_specs SEMI
    |   field_specs SEMI variant_dcl
    |   variant_dcl
    ;
id_colon_frob:
        IDENTIFIER COLON
    ;
variant_dcl:
        CASE_KW IDENTIFIER COLON simple_type_exp OF_KW union_components
        | id_colon_frob CASE_KW IDENTIFIER COLON simple_type_exp OF_KW
            union_components
    ;
field_specs:
        field_spec
    |   field_specs SEMI field_spec
    ;
field_spec:
        field_id_list attributed_type
    |   field_attrs field_id_list attributed_type
    ;
field_attrs:
        attribute_opener field_attr_list attribute_closer
    ;
field_attr_list:
        field_attr
    |   field_attr_list COMMA field_attr
    ;
```

```
field_attr:
        LAST_IS_KW LPAREN IDENTIFIER RPAREN
    |   MAX_IS_KW LPAREN IDENTIFIER RPAREN
    ;
field_id_list:
        id_colon_frob
    |   field_id COMMA field_id_list
    ;
field_id:
        IDENTIFIER
    ;
union_components:
        union_component
    |   union_components union_component
    ;

union_component:
        union_tag COLON LPAREN field_specs RPAREN SEMI
    |   union_tag COLON LPAREN field_specs SEMI RPAREN SEMI
    |   union_tag COLON LPAREN RPAREN SEMI
    |   union_tag COLON IDENTIFIER COLON LPAREN field_specs RPAREN SEMI
    |   union_tag COLON IDENTIFIER COLON LPAREN field_specs
            SEMI RPAREN SEMI
    |   union_tag COLON IDENTIFIER COLON LPAREN RPAREN SEMI
    ;
union_tag:
        tag
    |   union_tag COMMA tag
    ;
tag:
        const_exp
    ;
proc_ptr_type_exp:
        HAT PROCEDURE_KW parameter_list
    |   HAT PROCEDURE_KW
    ;
func_ptr_type_exp:
        HAT FUNCTION_KW parameter_list COLON type_exp
    ;
string0_type_exp:
        STRING0_KW LBRACKET const_exp RBRACKET
    ;
proc_def:
        proc_header IDENTIFIER SEMI proc_options
    |   proc_header IDENTIFIER parameter_list SEMI proc_options
    ;
proc_header:
        routine_attribute_list PROCEDURE_KW
    |   PROCEDURE_KW
    ;
```

```
proc_options:
        list_directed_options
    |   option_directed_options
    |   /* nothing */
    ;
list_directed_options:
        list_option_element
    |   list_directed_options list_option_element
    ;
list_option_element:
        IDENTIFIER SEMI
    ;
option_directed_options:
        OPTION_KW LPAREN options_list RPAREN SEMI
    ;
options_list:
        IDENTIFIER
    |   options_list COMMA IDENTIFIER
    ;
func_def:
        function_header IDENTIFIER COLON type_exp SEMI
    |   function_header IDENTIFIER parameter_list COLON type_exp SEMI
    ;
function_header:
        routine_attribute_list FUNCTION_KW ;
    |   FUNCTION_KW
    ;
routine_attribute_list:
        attribute_opener routine_attributes attribute_closer
    ;
routine_attributes:
        routine_attribute
    |   routine_attributes COMMA routine_attribute
    ;

routine_attribute:
    |   IDEMPOTENT_KW
    |   MAYBE_KW
    |   BROADCAST_KW
    ;
parameter_list:
        LPAREN parameters RPAREN
    ;
parameters:
        parameter_spec
    |   parameters SEMI parameter_spec
    |   /* nothing */
    ;
parameter_spec:
        parameter_ids COLON attributed_type
    ;
```

```
parameter_ids:
        parameter_attrs parameter_id_list
    ;
parameter_id_list:
        parameter_id
    |   parameter_id_list COMMA parameter_id
    ;
parameter_id:
        IDENTIFIER
    ;
parameter_attrs:
        parameter_class attribute_opener parameter_attr_list
                attribute_closer
    |   parameter_class
    ;
parameter_attr_list:
        parameter_attr
    |   field_attr
    |   parameter_attr_list COMMA parameter_attr
    |   parameter_attr_list COMMA field_attr
    ;
parameter_attr:
        COMM_STATUS_KW
    |   IN_KW
    |   OUT_KW
    |   REF_KW
    ;
parameter_class:
        IN_KW REF_KW
    |   IN_KW OUT_KW
    |   IN_KW
    |   OUT_KW
    ;


c_interface_tail:
        c_interface_marker c_interface_body c_interface_close
    ;
c_interface_marker:
        LBRACE

    ;
c_interface_close:
        RBRACE

    ;
c_attribute_opener:
        LBRACKET

    ;

c_attribute_closer:
        RBRACKET

    ;
```

```
c_interface_body:
        c_exports
    |   c_imports c_exports
    |   /* nothing */
    ;
c_imports:
        c_import
    |   c_imports c_import
    ;
c_import:
        IMPORT_KW STRING SEMI
    ;
c_exports:
        c_export
    |   c_exports  c_export
    ;


c_export:
        c_type_dcl      SEMI
    |   c_const_dcl     SEMI
    |   c_operation_dcl SEMI
    ;

c_const_dcl:
        CONST_KW c_type_spec IDENTIFIER EQUAL c_const_exp
    ;
c_const_exp:
        INTEGER_NUMERIC
    |   IDENTIFIER
    |   STRING
    |   NIL_KW
    |   TRUE_KW
    |   FALSE_KW
    ;
c_type_dcl:
        TYPEDEF_KW c_type_declarator
    ;
c_type_declarator:
        c_attributed_type_spec c_declarators
    |   c_type_spec c_declarators
    ;
c_attributed_type_spec:
        c_attribute_opener c_type_attributes c_attribute_closer
c_type_spec
    ;
c_type_attributes:
        c_type_attribute
    |   c_type_attributes COMMA c_type_attribute
    ;
```

```
c_type_attribute:
        LAST_IS_KW LPAREN IDENTIFIER RPAREN
    |   MAX_IS_KW LPAREN IDENTIFIER RPAREN
    |   HANDLE_KW
    |   TRANSMIT_AS_KW LPAREN IDENTIFIER RPAREN
    ;
c_type_spec:
        c_simple_type_spec
    |   c_constructed_type_spec
    ;
c_simple_type_spec:
        c_floating_point_type_spec
    |   c_integer_type_spec
    |   c_char_type_spec
    |   c_boolean_type_spec
    |   c_byte_type_spec
    |   c_void_type_spec
    |   c_named_type_spec
    |   c_handle_type_spec
    |   c_drep_type_spec
    ;
c_constructed_type_spec:
        c_struct_type_spec
    |   c_union_type_spec
    |   c_enum_type_spec
    |   c_set_type_spec
    |   c_string0_type_spec
    ;

c_named_type_spec:
        IDENTIFIER
    ;
c_floating_point_type_spec:
        FLOAT_KW
    |   DOUBLE_KW
    ;

c_integer_size_spec:
        SMALL_KW
    |   SHORT_KW
    |   LONG_KW
    |   HYPER_KW
    ;
c_integer_modifiers:
        c_integer_size_spec
    |   UNSIGNED_KW
    |   UNSIGNED_KW c_integer_size_spec
    |   c_integer_size_spec UNSIGNED_KW
    ;
```

```
c_integer_type_spec:
        INT_KW
    |   c_integer_modifiers
    |   c_integer_modifiers INT_KW
    ;


c_char_type_spec:
        CHAR_KW
    ;
c_boolean_type_spec:
        BOOLEAN_KW
    ;
c_byte_type_spec:
        BYTE_KW
    ;
c_void_type_spec:
        VOID_KW
    ;
c_handle_type_spec:
        HANDLE_T_KW
    ;
c_struct_type_spec:
        STRUCT_KW c_struct_body
    ;
c_struct_body:
        LBRACE c_member_list RBRACE
    ;


c_union_type_spec:
        c_union_header LBRACE c_union_body RBRACE
    ;
c_union_header:
        UNION_KW SWITCH_KW LPAREN c_simple_type_spec IDENTIFIER RPAREN
    |   UNION_KW SWITCH_KW LPAREN c_simple_type_spec IDENTIFIER
            RPAREN IDENTIFIER
    ;
c_union_body:
        c_union_case
    |   c_union_body c_union_case
    ;
c_union_case:
        c_union_case_list c_member
    ;
c_union_case_list:
        c_union_case_tag
    |   c_union_case_list c_union_case_tag
    ;
```

```
c_union_case_tag:
      CASE_KW c_const_exp COLON
   ;
c_member_list:
      c_member
   |  c_member_list c_member
   ;

c_member:
      c_attributed_type_spec c_member_attribute_list
         c_declarators SEMI
   |  c_attributed_type_spec  c_declarators SEMI
   |  c_type_spec c_member_attribute_list c_declarators SEMI
   |  c_type_spec c_declarators SEMI
   ;
c_member_attribute_list:
      c_attribute_opener c_member_attributes c_attribute_closer
   ;
c_member_attributes:
      c_member_attribute
   |  c_member_attributes COMMA c_member_attribute
   ;
c_member_attribute:
      LAST_IS_KW LPAREN IDENTIFIER RPAREN
   |  MAX_IS_KW LPAREN IDENTIFIER RPAREN
   ;

c_enum_type_spec:
      ENUM_KW c_enum_body
   |  LONG_KW ENUM_KW c_enum_body
   |  SHORT_KW ENUM_KW c_enum_body
   ;
c_enum_body:
      LBRACE c_enum_ids RBRACE
   ;
c_enum_ids:
   |  c_enum_id
   |  c_enum_ids COMMA c_enum_id
   ;
c_enum_id:
      IDENTIFIER
   ;
c_set_type_spec:
      BITSET_KW c_type_spec
   |  LONG_KW BITSET_KW c_type_spec
   |  SHORT_KW BITSET_KW c_type_spec
   ;
c_string0_type_spec:
      STRING0_KW LBRACKET c_const_exp RBRACKET
   ;
```

```
c_declarators:
        c_declarator
    |   c_declarators COMMA c_declarator
    ;


c_declarator:
        c_simple_declarator
    |   c_complex_declarator
    ;

c_simple_declarator:
        IDENTIFIER

    ;
c_complex_declarator:
        c_pointer_declarator
    |   c_array_declarator
    |   c_function_ptr_declarator
    |   c_reference_declarator

    ;
c_pointer_declarator:
        STAR IDENTIFIER
    |   STAR CONST_KW IDENTIFIER
    |   CONST_KW STAR IDENTIFIER

    ;
c_reference_declarator:
        AMPER IDENTIFIER
    |   AMPER CONST_KW IDENTIFIER
    |   CONST_KW AMPER IDENTIFIER

    ;


c_array_declarator:
        IDENTIFIER LBRACKET RBRACKET
    |   IDENTIFIER LBRACKET STAR RBRACKET
    |   IDENTIFIER LBRACKET RBRACKET c_fixed_array_indices
    |   IDENTIFIER LBRACKET STAR RBRACKET c_fixed_array_indices
    |   IDENTIFIER c_fixed_array_indices

    ;
c_fixed_array_indices:
        c_fixed_array_index
    |   c_fixed_array_indices c_fixed_array_index

    ;
c_fixed_array_index:
        LBRACKET const_exp RBRACKET

    ;
c_function_ptr_declarator:
        c_function_ptr_hdr c_parameter_dcls

    ;
c_function_ptr_hdr:
        LPAREN STAR IDENTIFIER RPAREN

    ;
```

```
c_operation_dcl:
        c_routine_attribute_list c_simple_type_spec IDENTIFIER
          c_parameter_dcls
    |   c_simple_type_spec IDENTIFIER  c_parameter_dcls
    |   IDENTIFIER  c_parameter_dcls
    ;
c_routine_attribute_list:
        c_attribute_opener c_routine_attributes c_attribute_closer
    ;
c_routine_attributes:
        c_routine_attribute
    |   c_routine_attributes COMMA c_routine_attribute
    ;
c_routine_attribute:
    |   IDEMPOTENT_KW
    |   MAYBE_KW
    |   BROADCAST_KW
    ;

c_parameter_dcls:
        LPAREN c_param_list RPAREN
    ;
c_param_list:
        c_param_dcl
    |   c_param_list COMMA c_param_dcl
    |   /* nothing */
    ;
c_param_dcl:
        c_attributed_type_spec c_param_attribute_list c_declarator
    |   c_attributed_type_spec  c_declarator
    |   c_type_spec c_param_attribute_list c_declarator
    ;
c_param_attribute_list:
        c_attribute_opener c_param_attributes c_attribute_closer
    ;
c_param_attributes:
        c_param_attribute
    |   c_member_attribute
    |   c_param_attributes COMMA c_param_attribute
    |   c_param_attributes COMMA c_member_attribute
    ;
c_param_attribute:
        IN_KW
    |   OUT_KW
    |   COMM_STATUS_KW
    ;
%%
```

Appendix B

NCA Base Network Data Types

This appendix shows the interface definition file **nbase.idl,** which describes the NCA remote interface **nbase_.** The **nbase_** interface defines the basic network data types and constants used in NCA interface definitions, in NIDL/Pascal syntax.

```
%pascal


[uuid(339b18336000.0d.00.00.80.9c.00.00.00)] interface nbase_;

type
    binteger =
        0..255;                 { positive 8 bit integer }
    pinteger =
        0..65535;               { positive 16 bit integer }
    linteger =
        0..2147483647;          { positive 31 bit integer }

type
    status_$t =
        record
            all: integer32;
            end;

const
    status_$ok = 0;             { returned if called procedure
                                  is successful }
```

```
type
    uuid_$t =
        [handle] record
            time_high:   unsigned32;
            time_low:    unsigned;
            reserved:    unsigned;
            family:      byte;
            host:        array[1..7] of byte;
            end;

const
    socket_$unspec_port = 0;

type
    socket_$addr_family_t = (
        socket_$unspec,                 { Unspecified }
        socket_$unix,                   { Local to host (pipes, portals) }
        socket_$internet,               { Internetwork: TCP, UDP, etc }
        socket_$implink,                { ARPAnet imp addresses }
        socket_$pup,                    { PUP protocols: e.g. BSP }
        socket_$chaos,                  { MIT CHAOS protocols }
        socket_$ns,                     { Xerox NS protocols }
        socket_$nbs,                    { NBS protocols }
        socket_$ecma,                   { European computer manufacturers }
        socket_$datakit,                { Datakit protocols }
        socket_$ccitt,                  { CCITT protocols, X.25 etc }
        socket_$sna,                    { IBM SNA }
        socket_$unspec2,
        socket_$dds                     { Apollo DOMAIN/MSG protocol }
        );

const
    socket_$num_families = 32;          { maximum number of families you
                                          can define }

type

    { Generic socket address. ("struct sockaddr" from "sys/socket.h")
      Network address plus port (message queue within host). }

    socket_$addr_t = record
        family: socket_$addr_family_t;
        data:   array [0..13] of char;
        end;

    { Complete network address. Host & network ID. A "sockaddr" without
      the port. }

    socket_$net_addr_t = record
        family: socket_$addr_family_t;
        data:   array [0..11] of char;
        end;
```

{ Host identifier. Uniquely identifies a machine, but you may need
  to use a "socket_$net_addr_t" to actually talk to a machine. For
  some families (for example, Internet), the network address and
  host ID may be identical; for others (for example, NS), the host
  ID may be a strict subpart of the network address. }

```
    socket_$host_id_t = record
        family: socket_$addr_family_t;
        data:   array [0..11] of char;
        end;
end;
```

———— 🎛 ————

Appendix C

NCA Status Codes

This appendix shows the interface definition file **ncastat.idl,** which describes the remote interface **nca_status_**. The **nca_status_** remote interface consists of constant definitions for the NCA–defined status codes, in NIDL/Pascal syntax. NCA status codes are "well-known" and are part of the NCA/RPC protocol; that is, they are returned in *fault* or *reject* messages from servers. The first few status codes are derived from status codes that the Network Computing System (NCS) uses (NCS is Apollo's implementation of NCA.) Table 4–6 gives descriptions of these status codes.

```
%pascal

[uuid(3c667ff91000.0d.00.01.34.22.00.00.00)] interface nca_status_;

const
    nca_status_$comm_failure        = 16#1C010001;
    nca_status_$op_rng_error        = 16#1C010002;
    nca_status_$unk_if              = 16#1C010003;
    nca_status_$wrong_boot_time     = 16#1C010006;
    nca_status_$you_crashed         = 16#1C010009;
    nca_status_$proto_error         = 16#1C01000B;
    nca_status_$out_args_too_big    = 16#1C010013;
    nca_status_$server_too_busy     = 16#1C010014;
    nca_status_$unsupported_type    = 16#1C010017;
    nca_status_$zero_divide         = 16#1C000001;
    nca_status_$address_error       = 16#1C000002;
    nca_status_$fp_div_zero         = 16#1C000003;
    nca_status_$fp_underflow        = 16#1C000004;
    nca_status_$fp_overflow         = 16#1C000005;
    nca_status_$invalid_tag         = 16#1C000006;
    nca_status_$invalid_bound       = 16#1C000007;
end;
```

Appendix D

ASCII/EBCDIC Conversion Tables

This appendix gives tables for conversion between ASCII and EBCDIC character formats. Table D-1 shows ASCII-to-EBCDIC conversion. The codes in this table run from left to right, top to bottom. To locate the EBCDIC code that corresponds to a given 7-bit ASCII value (0-127), use the ASCII value as an index into the table.

Table D–1. ASCII–to–EBCDIC Conversion

0x00	0x01	0x02	0x03	0x37	0x2D	0x2E	0x2F
0x16	0x05	0x25	0x0B	0x0C	0X0D	0x0E	0x2F
0x10	0x11	0x12	0x13	0x3C	0x3D	0x32	0x26
0x18	0x19	0x3F	0x27	0x1C	0x1D	0x1E	0x1F
0x40	0x5A	0x7F	0x7B	0x5B	0x6C	0x50	0x7D
0x4D	0x5D	0x5C	0x4E	0x6B	0x60	0x4B	0x61
0xF0	0xF1	0xF2	0xF3	0xF4	0xF5	0xF6	0xF7
0xF8	0xF9	0x7A	0x5E	0x4C	0x7E	0x6E	0x6F
0x7C	0xC1	0xC2	0xC3	0xC4	0xC5	0xC6	0xC7
0xC8	0xC9	0xD1	0xD2	0xD3	0xD4	0xD5	0xD6
0xD7	0xD8	0xD9	0xE2	0xE3	0xE4	0xE5	0xE6
0xE7	0xE8	0xE9	0xAD	0xE0	0xBD	0x5F	0x6D
0x79	0x81	0x82	0x83	0x84	0x85	0x86	0x87
0x88	0x89	0x91	0x92	0x93	0x94	0x95	0x96
0x97	0x98	0x99	0xA2	0xA3	0xA4	0xA5	0xA6
0xA7	0xA8	0xA9	0xC0	0x4F	0xD0	0xA1	0x07

Table D–2 shows EBCDIC–to–ASCII conversion. The codes in this table also run from left to right, top to bottom. To locate the ASCII code that corresponds to a given 8–bit EBCDIC value, use the EBCDIC value as an index into the table.

0x20	0x01	0x02	0x03	0x3F	0x09	0x3F	0x10
0x3F	0x3F	0x3F	0x0B	0x0C	0x0D	0x0E	0x0F
0x10	0x11	0x12	0x13	0x3F	0x3F	0x08	0x3F
0x18	0x19	0x3F	0x3F	0x3F	0x3F	0x3F	0x3F
0x3F	0x3F	0x1C	0x3F	0x3F	0x3F	0x17	0x1B
0x3F	0x3F	0x3F	0x3F	0x3F	0x05	0x06	0x07
0x00	0x00	0x16	0x00	0x3F	0x1E	0x3F	0x04
0x3F	0x3F	0x3F	0x3F	0x14	0x15	0x00	0x1A
0x20	0x3F	0x3F	0x3F	0x3F	0x3F	0x3F	0x3F
0x3F	0x3F	0x3F	0x2E	0x3C	0x28	0x2B	0x7C
0x26	0x3F	0x3F	0x3F	0x3F	0x3F	0x3F	0x3F
0x3F	0x3F	0x21	0x24	0x2A	0x29	0x3B	0x5E
0x2D	0x2F	0x3F	0x3F	0x3F	0x3F	0x3F	0x3F
0x3F	0x3F	0x3F	0x2C	0x25	0x5F	0x3E	0x3F
0x3F	0x3F	0x3F	0x3F	0x3F	0x3F	0x3F	0x3F
0x3F	0x60	0x3A	0x23	0x40	0x27	0x3D	0x22
0x3F	0x61	0x62	0x63	0x64	0x65	0x66	0x67
0x68	0x69	0x3F	0x3F	0x3F	0x3F	0x3F	0x3F
0x3F	0x6A	0x6B	0x6C	0x6D	0x6E	0x6F	0x70
0x71	0x72	0x3F	0x3F	0x3F	0x3F	0x3F	0x3F
0x3F	0x7E	0x73	0x74	0x75	0x76	0x77	0x78
0x79	0x7A	0x3F	0x3F	0x3F	0x5B	0x3F	0x3F
0x3F	0x3F	0x3F	0x3F	0x3F	0x3F	0x3F	0x3F
0x3F	0x3F	0x3F	0x3F	0x3F	0x5D	0x3F	0x3F
0x7B	0x41	0x42	0x43	0x44	0x45	0x46	0x47
0x48	0x49	0x3F	0x3F	0x3F	0x3F	0x3F	0x3F
0x7D	0x4A	0x4B	0x4C	0x4D	0x4E	0x4F	0x50
0x51	0x52	0x3F	0x3F	0x3F	0x3F	0x3F	0x3F
0x5C	0x3F	0x53	0x54	0x55	0x56	0x57	0x58
0x59	0x5A	0x3F	0x3F	0x3F	0x3F	0x3F	0x3F
0x30	0x31	0x32	0x33	0x34	0x35	0x36	0x37
0x38	0x39	0x7C	0x3F	0x3F	0x3F	0x3F	0x3F

Glossary

acknowledgment (ack) packet

> An NCA/RPC packet that the client sends to the server to acknowledge receipt of a response to a non–idempotent request.

activity

> A thread of execution.

activity hint

> A packet header field (16–bit non–negative integer) that can be used to identify the client activity making the call.

activity identifier

> A UUID which uniquely identifies a client activity that is making a remote procedure call.

address family

> See **protocol family**.

application server

> The part of a distributed application that exports resources to client programs.

at most once operation

> An operation that cannot be executed more than once because it modifies state upon each execution. See also **non–idempotent operation**.

at most once protocol

> The NCA/RPC request–response protocol that guarantees that a remote call is executed at most once; that is, zero or one times.

at most once request

> A request for a non–idempotent procedure (a procedure that cannot be executed more than once).

base network data types

The set of NCA–specified network data types defined in the interface definition file **nbase.idl**.

Berkeley UNIX socket abstraction

A network programming abstraction developed by the University of California at Berkeley that is communications protocol–independent and is based on the concept of sending and receiving datagrams.

big–endian integer representation

A type of integer representation in which the bytes of an integer are ordered in consecutive bytes from most–significant byte to least–significant byte.

binding

An association between a remote call and an object. See also **handle**.

broadcast attribute

The NIDL routine attribute that invokes the NCA/RPC broadcast request–response protocol when specified in an operation declaration.

broadcast FSM

The NCA/RPC client protocol finite state machine that handles client requests for idempotent remote procedure calls to be sent to all hosts on a local network.

broadcast/maybe FSM

The NCA/RPC client protocol finite state machine that handles idempotent remote procedure call requests to be sent to all servers on a local network from clients that do not expect to receive responses to their requests.

broadcast/maybe operation

An operation that specifies the NIDL routine attributes **broadcast** and **maybe** and uses the NCA/RPC broadcast/maybe protocol.

broadcast/maybe request

A request for an idempotent procedure to which the client does not expect a response and which is to be sent to all servers in the network.

broadcast operation

An operation that specifies the NIDL **broadcast** routine attribute and uses the NCA/RPC broadcast protocol.

broadcast request

A request for an idempotent procedure that is to be sent to all servers in the network.

byte stream

A sequence of bytes indexed by non–negative integers.

byte type (NDR)

An 8–bit NDR transmissible type that passes uninterpreted from sender to receiver.

callback

> A remote procedure call that a server makes to a client when it has no information about the client and the client has requested a non–idempotent operation.

callback mechanism

> The protocol that NCA/RPC defines to enforce the "at most once" rule for non–idempotent remote procedure execution. See also **at most once protocol**.

canonical data conversion

> A method of handling heterogeneous data representations in which a single scalar data representation format is accepted as the standard data representation format by all communicating machines.

client

> The software subsystem that implements the NCA/RPC request–response protocol on the calling machine.

client FSM

> The set of finite state machines that specify the client portion of the NCA/RPC request–response protocol.

client program

> The part of a distributed application that consumes the resources that application servers export.

connection–oriented protocol

> A communications (or ISO transport layer) protocol that guarantees message delivery between client and server. TCP/IP is an example of a connection–oriented protocol.

constant declaration (NIDL)

> The NIDL syntax that specifies a constant which the interface exports.

Conversation Manager

> An NCA–defined remote interface specified in NIDL that processes server callbacks.

data representation protocol

> A set of rules that define how structured values in an application program's interface are to be represented in a byte stream.

directional attributes

> NIDL parameter attributes that indicate to the client and server FSMs the direction in which an operation's parameters are to be passed.

distributed application

> An application that distributes both data and computation across a network of different machines.

execution engine

The model for the execution of a remote operation on the server. The execution engine performs computations on the NCA/RPC server FSM's behalf and returns results (if any) as notification input to the server FSM.

execution engine notification input

The input to the server FSM that occurs as a result of a server FSM call to the execution engine. Execution engine notification indicates that the execution engine has changed its state.

explicit handle

A handle that is defined as the first parameter of an operation; the client supplies a value for the handle parameter each time it calls the operation.

fault packet

An NCA/RPC packet that the server sends to the client if the remote call received a fault while executing on the server side. The fault packet contains the fault status that corresponds to the fault that occurred.

field attributes

NIDL type attributes that can be applied to open arrays within records/structures or parameter lists. NIDL field attributes currently consist of the **last_is** and **max_is** attributes.

fixed array (NDR)

An ordered, one-dimensional, homogeneous, indexed collection of values whose type and number of elements are specified in the NIDL array type definition.

format label

A 4-byte data structure that identifies the data representation formats being used to represent scalar values in an NDR byte stream. Data representation format is established dynamically when an application makes a remote procedure call.

fragment

A packet that is part of a multi-packet transmission.

fragment acknowledgment (fack) packet

An NCA/RPC packet that the client sends to the server after it receives one fragment of a multi-packet response; or, a packet that the server sends after it receives one fragment of a multi-packet client request.

fragment number

A packet header field (16-bit non-negative integer) that identifies a packet when it is part of a multi-packet transmission.

FSM

Finite State Machine.

FSM action

> An action that is executed as a result of a client FSM or server FSM state transition. Steps within an action are represented as primitive global variable assignments and/or calls to client and/or server primitives.

FSM client action input

> Client FSM input that consists of 1) a request for a remote call or 2) a request to terminate a remote call in progress.

FSM input bundles

> The structured bundles of data associated with NCA/RPC FSM message, client action, and server execution engine notification inputs.

FSM message input

> Client FSM or server FSM input that coincides with the arrival of NCA/RPC packets.

FSM notation

> The keywords and symbols used in NCA/RPC FSM state transition and action tables and text.

FSM state transition (NCA)

> The tuple: [state, input, condition, new state, action].

FSM timeout input

> Client FSM and server FSM inputs that occur after a certain amount of time has passed in a state with no other inputs.

GLB database

> The database manipulated by the GLB.

Global Location Broker (GLB)

> The portion of the NCA Location Broker mechanism that maintains information about objects and interfaces throughout the network.

handle

> An implementation–defined specification of an object's UUID and location that the NCA/RPC protocol requires in order to deliver a remote call to its intended destination. A handle represents a binding between an object and a remote call (see also **binding**).

handle attribute

> The NIDL type attribute that identifies a type declaration as a non–primitive, user–defined handle.

handle_t type

> The NIDL simple data type that represents a primitive handle.

heterogeneous interconnect

> The layer of NCA that provides the basic interconnection among heterogeneous systems.

host identifier

A network address that uniquely identifies a particular machine.

idempotent attribute

The NIDL routine attribute that invokes the NCA/RPC idempotent request–response protocol when specified in an operation declaration.

idempotent operation

An operation that can be executed more than once because each execution modifies no state. An idempotent operation is declared with the NIDL **idempotent** routine attribute and uses the NCA/RPC idempotent request–response protocol.

idempotent request

A request for an idempotent operation.

implicit handle

A handle that is specified as a global variable by using the **implicit_handle** interface attribute. A handle specified with the **implicit_handle** attribute is used as the handle for all of the operations in the interface.

implicit_handle attribute

The NIDL interface attribute that identifies an implicit handle; that is, the handle to be applied to all operations in the interface.

import declaration

The NIDL syntax that specifies the name of a NIDL interface definition that defines constants and data types that the importing interface uses.

interface

A set of related operations.

interface definition

A structure written in NIDL that completely defines a remote interface, including constant declarations, type declarations, and the declarations for any operations to which clients can make remote calls. See also **remote interface**.

interface definition file

A file that specifies an interface definition.

interface header

The portion of a NIDL interface definition that contains the NIDL syntax identifier (NIDL/Pascal or NIDL/C), an interface attribute list, and the interface name.

interface hint

A packet header field (16–bit non–negative integer) that can be used to indicate which interface within a server a client is calling.

interface identifier

A UUID that uniquely identifies the interface that a client is calling.

interface specification

The interface ID, interface version number, and port vector combination. The interface specification uniquely identifies an interface.

interface version

A packet header field (32–bit non–negative integer) that identifies the version number of the remote interface that a client is calling.

last_is attribute

The NIDL field attribute that permits client and server to specify array size dynamically.

little–endian integer representation

A type of integer representation in which the bytes of an integer are ordered in consecutive bytes from least–significant byte to most–significant byte.

LLB database

The database manipulated by the LLB protocol.

LLB forwarding port

The well–known port specification at which servers exporting the LLB interface are to listen. The LLB forwarding port is defined in the NCA interface definition file **llb.idl**.

Local Location Broker (LLB)

The portion of the NCA Location Broker mechanism that maintains information about objects and interfaces on the local host.

max_is attribute

The NIDL field attribute that allows the client to indicate the maximum possible size of an array.

maybe attribute

The NIDL routine attribute that invokes the NCA/RPC maybe request–response protocol when specified in an operation declaration.

maybe FSM

The NCA/RPC client protocol finite state machine that handles idempotent remote procedure call requests from clients that do not expect to receive responses.

maybe operation

An operation that uses the NCA/RPC maybe request–response protocol.

maybe request

A request for an idempotent procedure to which the client does not expect a response.

multicanonical data conversion protocol

A method of handling heterogeneous data representations in which a set of scalar data representation formats is accepted as the set of standard representation formats by all communicating machines.

multi-threading

> A method of handling multiple activities simultaneously; for example, a server that implements multi-threading can process multiple remote procedure calls simultaneously.

natural alignment

> The alignment of scalar values of size 2^n at a byte stream index which is a multiple of 2^n, up to some limiting value of n.

NCA Location Broker (NCA/LB)

> The NCA-defined mechanism that provides clients with information about the locations of objects and interfaces.

NCA Remote Procedure Call (NCA/RPC)

> The Network Computing Architecture's implementation of the Remote Procedure Call mechanism.

network address

> A value that uniquely identifies a particular host on a network, given the protocol family.

network broker

> A software subsystem that provides information about available resources, both locally and network wide, and which acts as an intermediary between client programs requesting resources and application servers that provide access to those resources. The NCA/LB is an example of a network broker.

Network Computing Architecture (NCA)

> An architecture developed by Apollo for use in building distributed applications.

Network Data Representation (NDR)

> An NCA-defined data representation protocol that defines how the structured values supplied in a call to a remote interface are to be encoded into byte stream format for network transmission via NCA/RPC.

Network Interface Definition Language (NIDL)

> An NCA-defined language designed for the specification of interfaces to be invoked through the NCA/RPC mechanism.

network status codes

> The set of NCA status messages returned by NCA components. Network status codes are defined in the interface definition file **ncastat.idl**.

NIDL/C

> The NIDL grammar that is a subset of the ANSI C language with additional constructs to support the remote procedure call mechanism.

NIDL/Pascal

> The NIDL grammar that is a subset of the Pascal language with additional constructs to support the remote procedure call mechanism.

nocall packet

An NCA/RPC packet that the server sends to the client as a reply to a client ping packet. A nocall packet indicates that the server has no record of the client's request in its database.

non–idempotent operation

An operation that cannot be executed more than once because it modifies state upon each execution. See also **at most once operation**.

non–idempotent protocol

The NCA/RPC request–response protocol that guarantees that a remote call is executed at most once; that is, zero or one times. See also **at most once protocol**.

non–primitive handle

A handle that contains UUID and location information in a format that is meaningful to users and application programs. Non–primitive handles are identified by the NIDL **handle** type attribute.

object

A storage container; a disk file; a process.

object identifier

A UUID that uniquely identifies the object to which a client call is referring, if the call is operating on an object.

object–oriented architecture

An architecture that is based on the concept of objects, object types (or classes), and operations.

object type

A category of objects with similar characteristics.

open array (NDR)

An ordered one–dimensional, homogeneous collection of data whose type is specified in the NIDL array type definition but whose maximum and actual number of elements varies.

open record (NDR)

A non–variant record whose last field is either an open array or another open record.

operation

A procedure or a function.

operation attribute

See **routine attributes**.

operation declaration

The NIDL syntax that specifies a procedure and/or function that the interface exports, including procedure or function name, the type of function result returned (if any), and the types of all parameters to be passed in a call to the operation.

operation number

> A packet header field (16-bit non-negative integer) that identifies a particular operation within an interface. Operations in an interface are numbered in the order in which they are defined in the interface, starting with zero.

packet

> An NCA/RPC data structure that specifies how NCA/RPC request and response messages are structured.

packet body

> The portion of an NCA/RPC packet that contains the remote call's input or output arguments.

packet flags field

> A packet field (8-bit non-negative integer) that contains bit flags used for NCA/RPC client and server FSM protocol control.

packet header

> The portion of a packet that contains NCA/RPC protocol control information.

packet type field

> A packet header field (8-bit non-negative integer) that identifies the kind of request the client is making or the kind of response the server is returning.

ping packet

> An NCA/RPC packet that the client sends to the server when it wants to inquire about the status of an outstanding request.

port

> A socket message queue within a particular host.

port attribute

> The NIDL interface attribute that gives the port specifications for the interface.

port number

> The number that distinguishes a port from other ports within a host.

port specification

> The NIDL syntax that identifies the well-known port or ports on which servers that export the interface will listen.

primitive handle

> An implementation-defined specification of an object's UUID and location in a format that is meaningful to the client and server FSMs. Primitive handles are identified by the NIDL **handle_t** type.

protocol family

> A set of related protocols; for example, Sequenced Packet Protocol (SPP) and Packet Exchange Protocol (PEP) are related protocols because they are both part of the Xerox Network Systems (XNS) protocol family.

protocol family identifier

> A small number assigned by the University of California at Berkeley that specifies the communications protocol that created the network address of a host.

protocol version number

> A packet header field (16–bit non–negative integer) that identifies the version of NCA/RPC in use.

quit acknowledgment (quack) packet

> An NCA/RPC packet that the server sends to the client in response to a client quit packet which indicates that the server has aborted processing the remote call.

quit packet

> An NCA/RPC packet that the client sends to the server when it has incurred a quit fault. The quit packet instructs the server to abort processing of the client's remote call request.

record (NDR)

> An ordered, possibly heterogeneous collection of data whose types and number are specified in the NIDL record type definition.

reference attribute

> The NIDL/Pascal parameter attribute that indicates that the parameter is passed by reference from the client to the server.

reject packet

> An NCA/RPC packet that the server sends to the client when it has rejected the client's request.

remote interface

> A collection of related callable operations that are not necessarily local to the program that is calling them. See also **interface definition**.

Remote Procedure Call (RPC)

> The ability to call a procedure implemented in a server on a remote machine as if the procedure were local to the calling program.

request packet

> An NCA/RPC packet that the client sends to the server when it wants to execute a remote call. A request packet contains a packet header and the input arguments required by the remote procedure.

request–response protocol

> A client/server communications protocol in which a client sends a request and a server returns a response to the request.

response packet

An NCA/RPC packet that the server sends to the client if the procedure executed success-fully. A response packet consists of the packet header and the output arguments generated by the remote procedure execution.

routine attributes

The NIDL attributes that specify which protocol the NCA/RPC client and server FSMs are to use.

send–await–reply (SAR) FSM

The NCA/RPC client protocol finite state machine that handles client requests for idempotent and non–idempotent ("at most once") remote procedure execution.

sequence number

A packet header field (32–bit non–negative integer) that identifies the remote call that a client activity is making. All NCA/RPC messages issued on behalf of a single remote call will have the same sequence number, whether the messages are from client to server or server to client.

server

The software subsystem that implements the NCA/RPC request–response protocol on the machine that implements the target remote procedure.

server boot time

A 32–bit non–negative integer that indicates the time at which a server last booted. Server boot time indicates the time at which a given incarnation of a server processed its first remote call, not the time at which the machine on which the server is running last booted.

server FSM

The finite state machine that specifies the server portion of the NCA/RPC request–response protocol.

server support tools

Packages of subroutines that simplify the development of complex applications in a distrib-uted environment. Examples of server support tools include data replication tools and concurrent atomic transaction tools.

socket

An endpoint of communications in the form of a message queue.

socket address

A data structure that uniquely identifies a socket. An NCA socket address is an opaque data structure that consists of a protocol family identifier and a stream of bytes that con-tains a network address and a port number; it is defined as the type **socket_$addr_t** in the interface definition file **nbase.idl**.

source address

The socket address of a message sender.

transmissible type

A scalar type that can be passed in an NDR byte stream.

transmit_as attribute

The NIDL type attribute that associates a presented type, which clients and servers manipulate, with an NDR transmissible type, which is passed in the NDR byte stream.

type declaration (NIDL)

The NIDL syntax which specifies a type definition that the interface exports.

type attributes

NIDL syntax that modifies type expressions. NIDL type attributes currently include the **handle, transmit_as, last_is,** and **max_is** attributes. See also **field attributes**.

unreliable datagram service

A communications (or ISO transport) protocol in which message delivery between client and server is not guaranteed.

Universal Unique Identifier (UUID)

A fixed–length, 16–byte identifier that is guaranteed to refer to one entity (object, interface, or operation) for all time.

uuid attribute

The NIDL interface attribute that specifies the UUID that uniquely identifies the interface.

variant record (NDR)

An ordered, possibly heterogeneous collection of data whose types and number are specified in the NIDL record definition, but whose actual fields and number vary.

varying array (NDR)

An ordered, one–dimensional, homogeneous collection of data whose type and maximum number of elements are specified in the NIDL array type definition, but whose actual number of elements varies.

version attribute

The NIDL interface attribute that identifies the version number of the interface.

well–known port

A port that has been specially designated for communication between clients and servers; the port number assigned to a well–known port is identical across all hosts.

working packet

An NCA/RPC packet that the server sends to the client as a reply to a client ping packet. A working packet indicates that the server is processing the remote call.

zero–terminated string (NDR)

An open array of characters whose last element is a 0 byte.

Index

primitive, 97 to 98, 101, 196
in parameter declaration, 111
role in remote call, 114 to 115
specifying, 92
structure, 92

handle_t type, 101, 191

handling multiple clients, 63

heterogeneous interconnect, 1, 2, 191
components, 3

host identifier, 10, 179, 192

I

IBM floating–point representation, 126 to 127
conversion rule for, 127

idempotent
attribute, 110, 192
operation, 4, 192
request, 192
packet, 29

IEEE floating–point representation, 122 to 123
conversion rule for, 122

implementations, multi–threaded, 4

implicit handle, 92, 192
role in remote call, 115 to 116

implicit_handle attribute, 92, 192

import declaration, 89, 92 to 93, 192

integer
representation
and bit layout, 22
big–endian, 22, 119 to 120, 188
little–endian, 22, 119 to 120, 193
types
NDR, 119
NIDL, 100

interface, 5, 192
attribute list, 89
body, 89
definition file, 192
header, 89, 192
hint, 26, 192
identifier, 25, 192
name, 89
and object type, 9
specification, 45, 90, 193
syntax identifier, 89
version, 26, 193

interface attributes, 90 to 92
implicit_handle, 92
port, 91
syntax for declaring, 90
uuid, 91
version, 91

interface definition, 5 to 6, 87, 192
importing, 92 to 93
NCA–defined, 6
and NCA/RPC, 5
and NDR byte stream, 5
role in remote call, 114
structure, 88 to 89

K

KillApplicationProcedure primitive, 76

L

last_is attribute, 112 to 113, 193
and open array type, 107

lb_$entry_t fields, 143

little–endian integer representation, 22, 119 to 120, 193

LLB
constants, 141
data types, 142
database, 136, 193
adding to, 153 to 154
deleting from, 155 to 156
finding entries in, 157 to 159
error codes, 144
forwarding port, 58, 140, 193
interface definition, 6, 138 to 139, 140
operations, 140, 153
port specification, 140
See also LLB forwarding port

llb.idl, 6, 138 to 139

llb_$delete, 155 to 156

llb_$insert, 153 to 154

llb_$lookup, 157 to 159

Local Location Broker. *See* LLB

Location Broker. *See* NCA/LB

M

mapping
 arrays, 108
 multi-dimensional arrays, 128
 presented types to transmissible types, 97
 typed values to byte stream, 117

max_is attribute, 112 to 113, 193

maybe
 attribute, 110, 193
 FSM, 41, 54, 193
 operation, 193
 request, 193
  packet, 29

multi-threading, 4, 194

multicanonical data conversion, 8, 193

N

named type, NIDL, 101

natural alignment, 7, 194
 effect on NCA/RPC packet, 7
 and NDR byte stream, 118

nbase.idl, 6, 11, 177 to 179

NCA, x, 1 to 3, 194
 base network data types, 6, 177 to 179
 client-server model, 2
 data representation, 6 to 8
 fundamentals, 9
 interface definitions
  conv.idl, 82
  glb.idl, 136 to 138
  llb.idl, 138 to 139
  nbase.idl, 177 to 179
  ncastat.idl, 181
 Network Interface Definition Language, 5
  to 6, 87 to 115
  See also NIDL
 network
  broker architecture, 8
  model, 3, 13 to 18
 object orientation, 9 to 11
 overview, 1 to 8
 packet types, 23
 protocol
  family identifiers, 16
  NCA/LB, 135 to 144
  NCA/RPC client, 41 to 55
  NCA/RPC packet, 19
  NCA/RPC server, 63 to 75

NDR, 117 to 133
 NIDL, 87 to 115
reject status codes, 31
remote
 interfaces, 6
 procedure call, 3 to 5
  See also NCA/RPC
 and the socket abstraction, 14
 socket address data type, 15
 status codes, 6, 181
 structure, 1
 UUID data type, 10 to 12

NCA/LB, 8, 194
 constants, 141 to 144
 data types, 141 to 144
 error codes, 144
 GLB component, 135
 interface definitions, 6
 LLB component, 136
 operations, 144
 overview, 8
 protocol specification, 135 to 144

NCA/RPC, 3, 194
 callback mechanism, 5
 client, 4
  FSM, 41 to 55
 components, 3
 and the object model, 9 to 10
 packet definition, 19 to 32
 protocol
  at most once, 4 to 5
  client, 41 to 55
  fragmentation, 4
  idempotent, 4
  request-response, 3 to 4, 33
  server, 63 to 75
  summary, 4 to 7
 remote call semantics, 4 to 5
 server, 4
  FSM, 63 to 75

NCS (Network Computing System), xi

NDR, 3, 117 to 133, 194
 aggregate types, 128 to 132
 boolean type, 118
 byte stream, 7
  and NIDL interface definition, 5
 character type, 118
 constructed types, 128 to 132
 data
  conversion protocol, 7 to 8
  representation protocol, 7
 fixed array type, 128, 190

floating–point
    conversion chart, 121
    representation, 121 to 127
    types, 121 to 127
format label, 8, 133
integer
    representation format, 119 to 120
    types, 119
and natural alignment, 7
open array type, 128 to 129, 195
    and NIDL open array, 129
open record type, 131, 195
overview, 6 to 8
record type, 130
transmissible types, 118 to 128
variant record type, 130 to 131, 199
varying array type, 129 to 130, 199
zero–terminated string type, 132, 199

network
    address, 15, 179, 194
    broker, 1, 2, 8, 194
    status codes, 6, 181, 194

Network Computing Architecture. *See* NCA

Network Computing System, xi

Network Data Representation. *See* NDR

Network Interface Definition Language. *See* NIDL

NIDL, 3, 194
    array types, 107 to 109
    boolean type, 101
    byte type, 101
    character type, 101
    comm_status attribute, 114
    constant declaration, 93 to 94, 189
    constructed types, 102 to 109
    directional attributes, 113, 189
    enumerated types, 104 to 105
    field attributes, 112 to 113, 190
    floating–point types, 101
    function pointer type, 107
    grammar, 87 to 115
    handle attribute, 191
    handle_t type, 101, 191
    idempotent attribute, 192
    implicit_handle attribute, 192
    import declaration, 92 to 93
    integer types, 100
    last_is attribute, 193
    max_is attribute, 193
    maybe attribute, 193
    named type, 101

operation declaration, 109 to 116
overview, 5 to 6
parameter
    attributes, 112 to 114
    declaration, 111 to 114
pointer type, 106 to 107
record type, 104
reference
    attribute, 114, 197
    pointer, 107
relationship to NDR, 117
routine attributes, 110 to 111, 198
semantics, 87 to 115
set type, 105 to 106
simple types, 98 to 102
string0 type, 106
struct type, 103
subrange type, 105
syntax, 87 to 115
    notation, 87 to 88
transmit_as attribute, 199
type
    attributes, 96 to 98, 199
    declaration, 94 to 109, 199
union type, 103
version attribute, 199
void type, 101
yacc grammar, 161 to 176

NIDL/C, 194

NIDL/Pascal, 194

nocall packet, 4, 30, 195

non–idempotent
    operation, 4, 195
        handling a request for, 81 to 82
    protocol. *See* at most once protocol

non–primitive handle, 97 to 98, 195
    role in remote call, 115

notation, NIDL EBNF, 87 to 88

O

object, 9, 195
    identifier, 25, 195
    location information, 45
    model and NCA, 9 to 10
    type, 9, 195

object–oriented architecture, 195

open
- array
  - NDR, 128 to 129, 195
  - NIDL, 107
  - and field attributes, 112 to 113
  - in structure/records, 103
- record
  - NDR, 131, 195
  - NIDL, 104

operation, 9, 195
- attribute. *See* routine attribute
- GLB, 145
- idempotent, 4
- LLB, 153
- number, 196
  - determining, 115
  - packet field, 26
- and object type, 9
- semantics of a remote call to, 114 to 116

operation declaration, 89, 109 to 116, 195
- function result type, 109
- identifier, 109
- parameter
  - determining, 115
  - list, 109, 111 to 114
- routine attributes, 109, 110 to 111
- syntax for declaring, 109

P

packet, 19, 196
- ack, 4, 28, 187
- body, 19, 196
  - determining contents of, 115
  - length field, 27
- client-initiated, 27 to 29
- fack, 28, 190
- fault, 30, 190
- fields
  - activity hint, 26
  - activity identifier, 25
  - body length, 27
  - data representation format label, 24 to 25
  - flags, 23 to 24, 196
  - fragment number, 27
  - interface hint, 26
  - interface identifier, 25
  - interface version, 26
  - object identifier, 25
  - operation number, 26

- packet type, 22 to 23, 196
- protocol version number, 22, 197
- sequence number, 26, 198
- server boot time, 25
- flags, 23
  - bundle data, 36
  - field, 196
- fragments, 27
- header, 19, 20 to 27, 196
  - bundle data, 35
- nocall, 4, 30, 195
- ping, 4, 28
- quack, 30, 197
- quit, 28, 197
- reject, 30, 197
- request, 4, 28, 197
- response, 4, 30, 198
- server-initiated, 29 to 30
- size, 19
- structure, 27 to 32
- type field, 22 to 23, 196
- values, preserving, 29
- working, 4, 30

parameter
- attributes, 112 to 114
  - **comm_status**, 114
  - directional, 113
  - field, 112 to 113
  - reference, 114
- declaration, 111 to 114
- list, 109

passing complex types, 97

ping packet, 4, 28, 196

pointer type, NIDL, 106 to 107
- in structure/records, 103, 106 to 107

port, 15, 196
- attribute, 91, 196
- number, 15, 196
- specification, 91 to 92, 196
  - LLB, 140
  - use in client FSM, 92
- well-known, 199

preserving packet values, 29

primitive handle, 98, 101, 196
- role in remote call, 114

protocol family, 13, 197
- identifier, 10, 14 to 17, 197
  - and port specification, 91 to 92

protocol version number, 22, 197

T

transmissible types
  associating with presented types, 97
  boolean, 118
  byte, 127
  character, 118
  floating–point, 121 to 127
  integer, 119 to 121

transmit_as attribute, 97, 199
  and pointers in structure/records, 103

type
  attributes, NIDL, 96 to 98, 199
    See also field attributes
    handle, 97 to 98
    syntax for declaring, 97
    transmit_as, 97
  declaration, NIDL, 89, 94 to 109, 199
  transmissible, 199

U

Universal Unique Identifier. *See* UUID

union type, 103

unreliable datagram service, 17 to 18, 199

user interfaces, and NCA, 1

UUID, 10 to 12
  advantages to using, 11
  attribute, 90, 91, 199
  base network data type, 10 to 12
  layout, 10

uuid_$nil, using
  in delete operations, 147, 155

in **lb_$entry_t** fields, 143
in lookup operations, 149, 157

uuid_$t data type, 10, 178

V

VAX floating–point representation, 123 to 125
  conversion rule for, 125
  fields, 125

variant record type
  NDR, 130 to 131, 199
  NIDL, 104

varying array
  NDR, 199
  relationship to NIDL array, 129

version attribute, 91, 199

void type, NIDL, 101

W

well–known port, 15, 91 to 92, 199

working packet, 4, 30, 199

Y

yacc grammar, NIDL, 161 to 176

Z

zero–terminated string, NDR, 132, 199